How to Help Your Child
Succeed at School

How to Help Your Child Succeed at School

Parenting and Primary Schooling
Working in Partnership

Juliet Neill-Hall

HELP YOURSELF

British Library Cataloguing in Publication Data
A record for this book is available from the British Library

ISBN 0 340 78527 6

Typeset in ACaslonRegular by Avon DataSet Ltd,
Bidford-on-Avon, Warwickshire

Printed and bound in Great Britain by
Bookmarque Ltd, Croydon, Surrey

The paper and board used in this paperback are natural recyclable products
made from wood grown in sustainable forests. The manufacturing processes
conform to the environmental regulations of the country of origin.

Hodder & Stoughton
A Division of Hodder Headline Ltd
338 Euston Road
London NW1 3BH
www.madaboutbooks.com

For my parents
Henry and Jeanette
with love and thanks

Contents

Acknowledgements

My thanks to my agent, William Neill-Hall, who encouraged me, and my publisher, Judith Longman, who believed in the project sufficiently to wait two years for it.

Introduction

As parents, we all want the best for our children. From the moment we become parents, we have a plan. It may be a subconscious plan, not necessarily thought out and reflected upon, but when asked, most parents will say that they want to raise stable, well-adjusted, happy individuals who can fulfil their potential in life, form good and lasting relationships and be law-abiding, contributing members of society. This is a big task to achieve between birth and eighteen years of age. Our parenting alone will not be sufficient: we must work in partnership with family, friends and our children's school environment to achieve our aim.

We know that the primary school they attend will be one of the foundation stones for our children's education, social development and future success in life. Children only have one chance at education, so we want to ensure they are given the best opportunities to be happy and motivated learners who ultimately fulfil their potential and go into life with good qualifications and sound skills. We also want them to make friends and have good relationships within their peer group.

School has a vast and lasting impact on the lives of children. Apart from home, school is the single most important place in the lives of most children. Children spend about 1,500 hours a year in school, so during the course of their primary school they will spend 10,500 hours learning a comprehensive and diverse range of skills. Good schools should be a community extension of family life, setting new challenges and providing experiences that can help the child meet them.

How does our choice of school influence the education our children will receive? What makes a good school? How can we know what our children are learning within the school environment? How can we work in partnership with schools to develop the all-important skills that our children will need to cope in life? How does our parenting complement what happens in school? This book seeks to answer some of these complex questions.

A wide, broad and sound education is vital in today's quick-moving, ever-changing, demanding society. The workplace needs an educated and flexible workforce that has the necessary skills to meet the demands of business, industry and professional expertise. However, education is not just about gaining the qualifications that will enable children to take up opportunities and make choices in later life. It is the tool by which we develop a whole range of important life skills, acquire knowledge, explore problems and find solutions.

Education can open the door to our creative talents be they art, music, drama or design. It can train, develop and hone sporting talent. It helps us towards an understanding of the world and the people who have inhabited it in the past and live in it now. It teaches us to mix with our peer group, accommodate and co-operate with others and work together in an effective way. It can ultimately show us the way forward to fulfilling our own personal potential and provide us with a lifelong capacity to learn. Education shapes young people for the rest of their lives.

Obviously not all educational experiences take place in the context of school. Children learn in their families, in their locality and in religious communities, and from the all-pervasive culture in which they live. Newspapers, magazines and comics, television, radio and computers have a key role to play in bringing information and understanding as well as the music, toys and fashion of the moment.

Foreign travel has expanded children's understanding of different cultures and environments. Museums and galleries have become more interactive and child-friendly. Children are taken out into both the local and wider environment to visit interesting sites and locations and to learn about their history and cultural inheritance. Many leisure centres have comprehensive sports programmes offering a wide range of sports for children and young people.

However, for the majority of children a large chunk of their educational experiences take place within the context of the school environment. Schools therefore have a huge impact on shaping our children's perceptions of the world and in training them up for adult life. We entrust them with the responsibility of teaching our children a wide range of skills and giving them a moral outlook on life that will, to some degree, determine their futures and the way they live their lives.

Therefore we need to feel confident that the schools we choose are able to do the job in the best way possible. We also need to be aware as parents how best to support our children to succeed in school and reach their individual potentials.

This book aims to help you as parents choose the right school and to help your children develop the necessary skills paramount for success at school. It will allow you to understand the nature and content of modern-day schooling and how you as a parent can complement learning and give support from home. Lastly, it will allow you to be confident in addressing any difficulties that may arise at school.

Juliet Neill-Hall

1

Choosing the right school

The first step to helping your child succeed at school is choosing the right school for him or her. You may have strong beliefs about your child attending the local community school and may be happy with what is on offer. You may live in a rural area where there is not much choice. However, for many parents, the business of choosing a school is an important decision that will take time and energy to research. If you do not know much about the education system this can be a daunting task.

There are around 35,000 maintained or voluntary aided schools in the United Kingdom which are in the process of educating 90 per cent of the nine million school-aged children in this country. Meanwhile, around 600,000 children are educated in private schools which are independent of local and national government. They are funded through fees charged to parents and from charitable foundations and trusts.

By law, statutory education must begin at five years old and local education authorities have a duty to provide all children with a school place no later than the start of the term after their fifth birthday. The transition from a pre-school setting or from being at home with a parent or carer to a primary or infant school is a big step in your child's life. Careful consideration needs to be given to a range of important issues as you search for the appropriate school where your child will flourish in his or her personal and intellectual development.

Traditionally, children enter full-time education in the term in which they turn five. Most schools now operate a morning or afternoon session for the 'rising fives' in the autumn and spring terms leading to full-time attendance for summer birthdays in the summer term.

Your local education authority will provide you with a list of its primary schools, including their admissions policies. If you live close to the border of a neighbouring local authority, it is wise to get a copy of their list as well. Depending on the area in which you live, primary education can come 'packaged' in different forms:

Infant school (four- or five-year-olds to seven-year-olds) followed by junior school (seven-year-olds to eleven-year-olds), or primary school (four- or five-year-olds to eleven-year-olds)

or:

First school (four- or five-year-olds to eight-year-olds) followed by middle school (eight-year-olds to thirteen-year-olds).

It is worth remembering that children will inevitably go through a transition period between Infant and Junior or First and Middle while they adapt to a new environment. It is important to assess both schools before making a decision, particularly if they are on different sites and have a different head teacher.

If you are keen for your child to attend a particular secondary school, it will be necessary to check that the primary school you have chosen acts as a 'feeder' school to that secondary school. This means your child will go up into secondary school with a firm group of friends, and be more likely to settle quickly.

Parental rights of choice in the state-maintained sector

Your right to state your preference of school is set out very clearly in the Education Act of 1980. You do not have to choose the nearest school, or, indeed, any school, within your local education authority boundaries. The law says that local education authorities must abide by parental choices unless there are particular reasons for not being able to comply with this, such as the school being full to capacity.

The Education Act 1980

- gives parents the right to state their choice of school;
- says education authorities must comply unless there are specific reasons not to do so and gives parents the right to appeal;
- makes the appeal verdict binding on the education authority and on the school.

The Education Reform Act 1980

- introduced 'open enrolment', preventing artificial limits on school numbers;
- set a 'standard number' of pupils for each school which reflects its physical capacity and requires schools to accept pupils up to that number;
- prevents education authorities discriminating against you just because you live across the border in another authority.

Each year, education authorities must publish details of their admissions arrangements. These must state how many pupils will be admitted and how places will be allocated if schools are over-subscribed. The most common criteria are:

- physical proximity to the school;
- siblings already attending the school;

- particular special need – for example, your child may have specific physical requirements that can only be met in one local school environment;
- Church schools will also require proof of the family's regular attendance and commitment to a local church. You will usually be asked for a written statement of support from your vicar, pastor or priest to confirm this.

In theory, therefore, parental choice allows you to apply for your child to attend any local authority school you want. In practice, choice can be limited to what is actually available. In rural areas, there are often fewer schools spread over a wide area and you have to consider the feasibility of actually getting your child there. In urban areas, choice can be restricted by the sheer weight of applications. This can be caused either by perceived popularity or a local dense young family population, so that schools are forced to determine their intake by application criteria. Church primary schools tend to be particularly oversubscribed as often they have a reputation for excellence and are popular with parents because of their moral and spiritual framework.

Gathering information

Your Local Education Authority will have the names, addresses and telephone numbers of all the educational establishments in your area, as well as the head teacher's name, the number of pupils on the roll, and the number to be admitted next year for each school. For further information, contact the schools you are interested in and ask for a prospectus.

There is now far more public information available to parents than ever before to help them make decisions about schools, and it is important to gather as much information as possible to help you. The next thing to do is to book appointments to make visits to see individual schools. The following are essential:

The school prospectus

The school prospectus/brochure usually covers the following areas:

- The aims and ethos of the school.
- General information on numbers, ages of pupils and accommodation, and the hours of the school day.
- Names of the governing body.
- A list of school staff.
- Whether or not there is an attached nursery class.
- Facilities within the school.
- Policies on equal opportunities and special needs.
- Policies on behaviour and bullying.
- Uniform policy.
- Policy on parental involvement in the school.
- A copy of the most recent SATs (Standard Attainment Tests – see page 10 for more information) results.
- A copy of GSCE or A level results (secondary school).

OFSTED report

OFSTED (The Office for Standards in Education), officially the Office of Her Majesty's Chief Inspector of Schools in England, is a non-ministerial government department, independent from the Department for Education and Employment.

The role of OFSTED is to improve standards of achievement and quality of education by carrying out regular independent inspection, public reporting and informed independent advice. It provides regular inspection of the 24,000 schools in England that are wholly or mainly state-funded. A similar system of inspection applies to all institutions that are in receipt of public funding, providing education for under four-year-olds.

OFSTED inspections look carefully at:

- the way pupils are taught;
- what the pupils achieve in their lessons;

- the school's test and examination results, especially in English, mathematics and science;
- how well the school provides for children with special educational needs;
- how the school is led and managed;
- pupils' attitudes and behaviour;
- the spiritual, moral, social and cultural development of pupils;
- how well the school cares for its pupils;
- how well the school works with parents;
- how satisfied parents are with what the school offers;
- the quality of lessons, clubs and other opportunities provided for pupils;
- the way in which financial resources are managed;

The report will lay out the main strengths and weaknesses of the schools and provide a range of advice on ways it can improve and move forward. The school must respond to the report with an Action Plan that can also be made available to parents.

Annual and OFSTED reports can be found in the local library, or be requested from the school itself. Alternatively, OFSTED reports can be found on the Internet at http://www.ofsted.gov.

Annual report of the school governors

This will give you up-to-date information on the progress of the school over the last year. It may outline some of the policies the school or setting has put in place since the last OFSTED report.

SATs performance

SATs (Standard Attainment Tests) are the government-promoted national tests in English, Mathematics and Science for seven- and eleven-year-olds. The tests are the same for all children in the age groups and are combined with in-school teacher assessments to evaluate both the progress of individual children and the overall performance of the school. Your local education authority will publish tables showing the results from all the primary schools in your area. These are published annually in local newspapers or can be found in your local library. You can then compare results both within the area itself and against a national average.

Many independent schools now take SATs tests in order to put themselves in context with mainstream education. These are not published in the local press but will be available from the school themselves.

Obviously, the school's SATs performance will give you an indication of the academic standards being achieved in school but it is worth bearing in mind that this is not the whole picture of how successful or otherwise a school is in educating young children. SATs performance will be influenced by other factors, such as the particular intake for that year, the area in which the school is situated, and the number of children with special educational needs which are being catered for. SATs results at eleven years old are more indicative of a primary school's overall performance than those at seven years old, because the school has had more chance to develop skills.

SATs results are best assessed in profile with the OFSTED report which will give you a better indication of the overall performance, strengths and weaknesses of a particular school.

Local community perspectives

These can be best gained through chatting to other local parents, asking neighbours' children if they like and enjoy their school, or asking others in your community such as the health visitor or church leader if they know anything about the quality of education at a particular school or what people 'say' about it.

This kind of hearsay is worth listening to in order to form an impression of 'customer satisfaction' but it is worth remembering that every parent has his or her own view of a school and what suits their child might not necessarily suit yours. One parent might have a particular grouse with the school about something while another is totally delighted with the music provision because her child is musical.

The visit

It is important to visit a selection of schools to get an overall impression of what is available. This can be very time-consuming, but it is only through visiting a school that you can get an in-depth impression of what it is like and what it has to offer. Schooling is of vital importance to children and you are entrusting a large proportion of your child's life into the hands of the staff in a particular school environment.

Some schools arrange open days when parents can come and get an impression of the school and the head teacher will often give a short address on its aims and ethos. These can be useful occasions for gaining a glimpse of a number of schools in action, but it is also important to visit a school individually, meet the head teacher on a one-to-one basis, and ask individual questions to evaluate the person whose opinions and management will be shaping your child's educational experience.

When you have decided to visit a school, contact them in plenty of time, at least a term before your child is due to enrol. Put aside at least an hour and a half to complete your visit so that you have a chance to have a really good look around, get a feel of the place, inside and out, and to ask the staff, particularly the head teacher, your questions. Make sure the children are in school so you will have the opportunity to see the organisation at work.

It is wise not to bring a young child with you on these visits. First, it is confusing for small children to visit a number of different environments to which they might be going. Second, it is difficult to concentrate and to accurately assess the situation with a little person tugging at your leg, especially if they start to misbehave just when you wish they wouldn't!

Ideally, both parents or guardians should visit together so you can discuss your impressions in detail afterwards. Alternatively, take another member of the family or a friend. It is helpful to take a notebook with a list of questions ready to ask and a pen to note down answers and any general views you might have.

Choosing an independent school

Children attending independent schools are statistically more likely to leave school with a greater number of qualifications, at better grades, and are more likely to gain entry to the top universities. However, it is extremely difficult to disentangle this from early selection of pupils on the grounds of ability or parental input and socio-economic factors. In other words, if you select a group of clever children from supportive backgrounds with well-educated parents who can afford extra resources, it is not surprising that they are likely to perform above average.

Parents usually consider independent education for the following reasons:

- A belief that educational standards will be higher.
- Strong religious beliefs.
- Smaller classes.
- Social reasons – wanting a child to mix with the 'right crowd'.
- General dissatisfaction with local state schools in the area.
- A belief that their child's particular needs will be best met in the independent sector.
- A family tradition.
- A wider range of facilities and sporting options.
- Boarding facilities.

It would be a mistake, however, to assume that just because a school is independent and charging fees it is necessarily offering a better standard of education than your local school. It is worth investigating all options before making your decision – or parting with your money. Independent school fees are very costly and out of the reach of most ordinary families; however, financial support may be available through scholarships and bursaries. If your child has a particular talent in music, art or sport, or is particularly academic, he or she may well have the opportunity to earn a scholarship or bursary to help with the fees.

In addition to the indicators mentioned in the state-maintained section, independent schools do have a slightly different inspection route than that followed by OFSTED. OFSTED contact with independent-aims schools is mainly in the form of one or two day inspection visits, for monitoring/registration purposes. These do not lead to any public documents. It carries out full inspections of a small number of independent schools, at the request of the DfES (Department for Education and Skills). These can be obtained from their publications centre (020 7510 0180).

Independent schools that belong to the Independent Schools Council (ISC) are inspected by the Independent Schools Inspectorate (ISI). From January 1999, the reports have been public documents available from the schools themselves. A school must pass an ISI accreditation inspection to qualify for membership of an association within ISC. Schools are evaluated within a framework agreed with OFSTED in relation to criteria covering:

- resources;
- administration;
- standards of achievement;
- organisation and management;
- quality of teaching and learning;
- curriculum;
- assessment;
- staffing;
- recording and reporting;
- premises.

Many independent schools in the primary sector divide themselves into two stages:

Pre-Preparatory (Pre-Prep) three- to seven-year-olds and Preparatory (Prep) seven- to thirteen-year-olds, or Junior three- or five- to eleven-year-olds.

The 'preparatory' traditionally refers to the two years, from eleven to thirteen, when prep school boys prepare for entry to a large public (in fact private) school through means of what is called the 'Common Entrance'. This is an exam in all areas of the curriculum, often to a very high standard, by which boys, in particular, enter the public school system.

What complicates the matter further is that girls' independent secondary schools have traditionally started at eleven rather than at thirteen. So girl-only independent schools will go from four or five years old to eleven years old.

As a large proportion of independent primary education is now co-educational, it is becoming increasingly common for private co-educational secondary schools to have a junior section from eleven to thirteen, so youngsters leave their primary education at eleven, but still take Common Entrance at thirteen. This also means that children who have been in the state-maintained sector can more easily fit in at eleven into the independent sector.

Many schools have a waiting list where children are put down, sometimes from a very early age, to attend the school in the future. Schools usually ask for some kind of token registration fee to do this. For some schools this is a guarantee of a place, but you need to check this as the pressure for places, particularly in large urban areas, is such that schools will use other methods to decide on which children gain entry at three, four or five years old.

Oversubscribed private schools, or those that wish to protect their high-achieving academic record, may select even very young children of three and four through a screening test. Children will spend a morning at the school in the reception class being observed playing and engaging with one another and doing simple tasks. The idea is to select youngsters who seem to show the most promise at simple problem-solving tasks, pre-literacy and pre-numeracy tasks, and who have a lively and alert general presentation. Children born between September and December have a natural advantage and can often pre-dominate private school entry when selected in this way.

At prep or junior school stage, children will be expected to take a written test in basic skills as well as an informal assessment and/or interview.

Most prep school prospectuses will outline which secondary schools their pupils have gone onto after leaving. This is something you need to investigate to see if they prepare pupils for the kind of school you would like your child to attend at eleven or thirteen. A prep school that sends children to a variety of different secondary education settings is a good sign. It indicates that the school is not only interested in academic achievement but also a breadth of education that values the potential of each individual child.

2

What makes
a good school?

In theory, all schools should be fairly similar. They all contain
teaching staff, support staff and pupils. It is also the case that with
the national curriculum in place, which outlines how and what
children should be taught at any given stage, schools are all
teaching very similar things. However, in reality, there is a huge
variety in the atmosphere, ethos (set of aims and principles that
govern direction), environment, teaching and learning, and in the
overall quality of the educational experience in different schools.
This happens even within schools in the same area with similar
intakes of young people. Why is this?

School organisations are living organisms in themselves – they
adapt, change and re-shape constantly. A whole range of factors
will influence the shaping of a school at any one time. Factors
such as the ethos and direction of the school, the efficiency with
which it is run, its financial management, together with the
resources it has available, and the quality of the staff all have a part
to play. The location of the school, be it inner city, suburban or
rural, and the socio-economic status of the pupil intake, also
influence outcomes.

However, good schools, as complex organisations, tend to have in place certain key factors which highlight them as effective establishments which are well thought of and which have good results. It is possible to break these down and look out for them when choosing a school.

Leadership and vision

Governing body

The governing body is, by law, in overall charge of a school, with the head teacher being responsible for the day-to-day management of the organisation. The governing body has wide-sweeping powers and considerable influence on the direction of the school. It is made up of the head teacher, at least one teaching member of staff, at least two parent governors, political representatives from the local authority (although these are not allowed to be in the majority), and other community members who may have a specialised knowledge or a particular interest. The numbers will vary according to the size of the school.

The governing body has a responsibility to:

- select and appoint staff, including the head teacher;
- offer support and direction to the head teacher;
- discipline and dismiss staff if necessary;
- decide how to spend the school's budget and keep accounts;
- make sure that the National Curriculum is in place and that assessment tests are carried out;
- make good provision for children with special educational needs;
- make decisions, in conjunction with the head teacher, regarding exclusion of pupils;
- ensure the law on religious education and collective worship is followed;
- draw up a policy on sex education;
- approve, monitor and moderate other school policies such as behaviour, bullying or equal opportunities.

A good governing body can clearly be a strong influence in the running of a school, and it is important to know who the members are and to have some idea of what their views are, particularly if they are political appointments.

Head teacher

A good head teacher is the most important influencing factor in an effective school. Schools' reputations rise and fall, depending on the ability and vision of the head teacher. The head teacher must have a clear vision as to what kind of school they want and be aware of the strategies they are going to use to go about achieving their aims.

The head has to communicate his or her vision to the school governors, school staff, parents and pupils in a way that fires their imaginations and commits them to his or her agenda.

Head teachers nowadays have tremendous demands put upon them by government initiatives and the complexity of the job. As well as being sound teachers who can communicate and deal with children in an effective way, they need to have considerable administrative skills and the financial expertise to run their own budgets.

It is generally believed that the most productive years of a headship are between three and seven years into the post. In the first three years, the head has had time to 'new broom' and to make changes to the staffing procedures and environment that he or she feels are necessary to put their own vision into place, and they are then able to build on and maintain these foundations with energy and high motivation. That is not to say that good head teachers do not remain very effective throughout their term of office.

Ethos and expectations

Most schools will lay out their main values and aims in their prospectus. This will give you an idea of the ethos that is being promoted within a particular school environment. It is very important that the school ethos matches your own priorities as to what you want for your child and the kind of environment within which you wish to place them. For example, if it is important to you that Christian values and teaching are promoted within a school, you should check that this is outlined in the ethos. Then, when you visit the school, enquire further and explore in exactly what way, and to what extent, this is done. Values and aims might, typically, be outlined using rather all-encompassing vague phraseology such as 'individuals matter', 'equality of opportunity', or 'high quality pastoral care'. It is important that these are not just empty words but that there are planned strategies in place to ensure that the wonderful-sounding values and aims are forged in the furnace of reality! When you visit the school, there should be evidence of the ethos in what you observe. Ask the head teacher specific questions relating to the ethos that you may have a particular interest in.

Environment

The environment of the school is known to have a direct relationship on school effectiveness. Pleasant surroundings with well-maintained buildings and outside areas have an effect on morale and esteem. Classrooms that are well-decorated and have colourful and well-thought-out displays engender an atmosphere where learning and pupil achievement are both recognised and valued.

Staff

The quality and commitment of the staff employed by the school will obviously have a direct bearing on the quality of education offered. Staff with good qualifications from recognised institutions who have continued to seek further training throughout their careers are an obvious requirement. It is good to have a mixture of age and experience. Young teachers bring in new ideas and innovations which are well-balanced by those who have established good practice over a number of years.

A high turnover of staff might indicate weak or over-dictatorial leadership, poor management, lack of resources or some other weakness in the fabric of the school. A staff group where there is never any change might make for a dull environment where new ideas and new blood are not revitalising practice.

The best teachers:

- are in the classroom to greet their pupils on arrival;
- know what they are teaching well;
- have something ready for pupils to do at the start of a session;
- plan lessons effectively with a clear learning goal;
- deliver the curriculum in an interesting and creative way;
- include a considerable portion of whole-class teaching in their lesson plan;
- use visual displays and involve children in practical activities;
- are organised and have the necessary equipment ready;
- value children's contributions;
- set appropriate homework and mark it quickly with good feedback;
- have a summary and wind-up session at the end of a lesson in which children can clarify what they have learned;
- are able to control the class successfully;
- are teaching good behavioural and learning skills as well as their subject;
- use a high level of positives to negatives to promote good behaviour and motivate pupils to produce good work;
- are firm but fair with regards to discipline;
- will differentiate the work set to accommodate pupils with special needs;
- are aware of any difficulties their pupils may be experiencing;
- give extra time when necessary;
- work closely with other colleagues;
- communicate with parents and work in partnership with them;
- speak to children with respect;
- have a sense of humour and proportion.

Curriculum and delivery

Schools do not have so much control over the curriculum – what is actually taught on a day-to-day basis – as they did in the past. What children learn and how they learn it is more directly controlled than ever before by central government, through the National Curriculum. Teachers have detailed training to help them deliver the National Curriculum in a comprehensive and, to a large extent, uniform way. Research has indicated that children learn most when taught as whole-class group. This is why large proportions of the 'literacy hour' and 'numeracy hour' in primary school are spent with the teacher talking and asking questions of the whole group. Pupils will then divide off into doing individual work or into ability or mixed-ability groups to tackle teacher-directed tasks.

The content of the curriculum is structured so that children are expected to have acquired a base level of knowledge and skills at each stage of their education. At the end of each stage, they are tested on this knowledge and skills by government set tests known as SATs (Standardised Attainment Tests). The stages are:

5–7 Years Key Stage 1
7–11 Years Key Stage 2

The core subjects of the National Curriculum are Mathematics, English, Science, and Welsh in Welsh-speaking schools in Wales. These are tested through SATs. The foundation subjects of History, Geography, Technology, Music, Art, Physical Education and Religious Education are also compulsory for all pupils. Every LEA is responsible for deciding the Religious Education syllabus in the area in consultation with their Standing Advisory Committee on Religious Education which must include representatives of all the main religious groups in the area, Christian and non-Christian. All schools must provide daily religious worship and religious teaching in schools should be mainly 'Christian in character'.

The daily act of worship – or religious assembly – remains compulsory for all pupils and should be mainly Christian in content. Individual assemblies may celebrate other world religions but they must not predominate. Parents are legally entitled to withdraw their child from both religious education and school worship if they see fit. Whole schools, too, can request permission to opt out of the requirement for mainly Christian worship. To do so, they must consult governors and parents and get permission from their local advisory committee. This might arise where a large proportion of pupils at school are from a minority religion.

Although schools can't control the content of the curriculum, good schools can influence the delivery of that curriculum by making sure that there are good resources in place – equipment, games, play materials, textbooks, videos, computer access and good library facilities. They can also make sure that their teachers have up-to-date training on how children learn most effectively and make sure they are delivering the curriculum in the way that is most likely to motivate and promote knowledge and skills.

For example, it is known each human being has a built-in, genetically predisposed tendency to learn most effectively in one of three ways. The first is through what we hear (auditory), the second through what we see (visual), and the third through what we do (kinaesthetic). So schools and teachers must make sure that as well as instructing children and teaching them verbally, every lesson must have visual input and practical application in order to engage all the youngsters in a particular group.

Attendance

Regular attendance at school is obviously an important factor in ensuring that children progress and do well at school. Good schools will promote an attendance policy which rewards good attendance and encourages children to see school as enjoyable and worthwhile.

Pastoral care

Effective schools will have supportive pastoral care. Although schools are primarily responsible for education, they also have a role to play in supporting children and young people who may be experiencing difficulties and problems in their home life. Education is also about the whole child. Bereavement, parental separation, unemployment, alcohol and drug abuse, as well as other life issues, all have an impact on children's educational opportunities. Children will often turn to teachers for a sympathetic ear and advice or to get help. Schools need to have a system of support with appropriate referral to senior staff when necessary.

Schools need to emphasise the importance of each individual being both listened to and heard when they need to be. Some primary schools will have 'listening' systems like Circle Time. This is a technique in which children sit in a circle, play games and talk and listen to one another about their feelings. During Circle Time each child will have an opportunity to give their thoughts and feelings on something. A typical 'round' (going round the circle) might be: 'A friend is someone who . . .' or: 'I feel happy when . . .' This encourages children to have the necessary language skills to be able to talk about their feelings and the ability to listen to others. Sometimes the Circle becomes a problem-solving Circle if there are issues about bullying or other poor behaviour in which children seek their own solutions to problems, supported by the teacher.

The behaviour policy

No effective learning can take place unless there is discipline and good order in the school environment. All schools are required to have a written Whole-School Behaviour Policy, available to be read by parents. How schools manage behaviour is a key indicator to overall performance. Schools with well-managed behaviour and pastoral care will engender good learning outcomes.

The most effective Whole-School Behaviour Policies put an overall emphasis on managing behaviour in a positive way. First, this means giving clear expectations as to how everyone in the school community is to behave in the classroom, playground and around the school. Second, these expectations need to be positively reinforced by staff regularly praising and rewarding pupils who conform to rules and routines. This way good behaviour becomes learned and habitual. Schools that put an emphasis on noticing and punishing poor behaviour may be reinforcing in the minds of young people the fact that bad behaviour is more likely to gain attention from the staff than good behaviour. Being negative can also lower self-esteem and create an unpleasant atmosphere.

For parents, this is a particularly pertinent issue as we want our children to learn good behaviour skills such as following instructions, listening, taking turns and co-operating with others. We also want their education to be free from disruption and interruption, so that they can get on with the business of learning and relating to one another socially.

Serious behaviour

Good schools will have a clear policy on how they will help children with emotional and behavioural difficulties, and on the kind of pastoral care they can offer. Many children go through difficult experiences in their lives, causing them to 'play out' their pain and insecurity through poor behaviour. It is vital for schools to be caring and supportive towards these young people and to help modify their poor behaviour and get them back on track. Some youngsters will need help from outside agencies: supportive schools will have a good relationship with educational psychologists, advisory teachers, educational welfare officers, social services and health professionals.

On the other hand, you want to be assured that if a pupil is being very disruptive or violent, your child will be protected from them. You need to ask how the school deals with more serious incidents of bad behaviour, such as bullying, and verbal or physical aggression. For example, what sorts of incidents would lead to a temporary or permanent exclusion?

Equal opportunities

All schools should have clear policies outlining how they will make sure that all members of the school community – whatever their gender, colour, race, religion or disability – are treated equally.

Special needs policy

A large proportion of children will have special educational needs at some time during their school career. As a rule, schools that are adept at managing special needs and helping children to reach their full potential tend to be schools which show high-quality provision overall. Schools interested in making sure the individual child flourishes and does his or her best will also be setting high standards and making healthy provision for all children.

Anti-bullying policy

Bullying in school can cause great unhappiness and distress to children. Schools are required to have whole-school anti-bullying policies that lay down expectations as to how people in the school environment should behave towards each other. They should outline not only ways in which the school tries to prevent bullying happening in the first place but also how it might tackle any bullying incidents. It is important to have a look at this and to make sure you agree with the way the school proposes to handle bullying if it occurs. Children should always be encouraged to report any incidents of bullying to an adult and this should not be regarded as 'telling tales'.

Parent–school partnership

Good schools work hard at cultivating a partnership with parents. Good communication about what is happening in school and how your child is progressing is essential. Parents want to feel they are part of the process of education and have a part to play, hand in hand with the school. If big decisions are being made about school buildings or structural development, then parents should be consulted and their views listened to. It is worth asking about a school's approach to this. Does it have a newsletter? How does it communicate with parents?

Reports on your child's progress

You will want to be regularly updated as to your child's progress in school. Different schools have different ways of talking to parents and keeping them informed. If you will be delivering and fetching your child from school, then there is often an opportunity for a quick update from your child's teacher, but if this is not possible because of work commitments, it is particularly important to ask how often there is a parents' evening when you will have an opportunity to talk to your child's teacher and to see your child's work. Schools are required to give a written report at least once a year, usually in the summer term.

Availability of staff if you have a problem

If there is a problem in school, you will want to be able to access a member of staff as quickly as possible. Make sure that the school has an 'open-access' system which means that you can talk to someone, usually the class teacher in the first instance, to sort things out.

Parental participation

The best primary schools welcome parents through the school doors with open arms (they have nothing to hide) and use them to help support pupils and the multitude of activities taking place at school. This might be through hearing a group of children read, preparing materials, or helping a small group to complete a task. Obviously, however, parents have to work strictly under the direction of the class teacher, and to respect confidentiality. Often, parents are asked to help out in a classroom other than the one their child attends. Sometimes, parents are asked to run after-school clubs like football or dance, according to their particular expertise.

Parent–Teacher associations

Many schools have active Parent–Teacher associations which arrange social events and raise money for the school. Schools with thriving PTAs reflect a good relationship between school and parents.

The school visit: what to look for on your visit

Children

The first priority is to discover how the children in the school appear to be engaging with one another, with members of staff and with the environment. Children should appear happy, well-motivated and well-behaved. They should be:

- happy – smiling, laughing, enjoying themselves;
- busy and motivated;
- absorbed in what they are doing;
- interacting with each other;
- lively and open;
- responding with trust to members of staff;
- following routines;
- polite, courteous and helpful.

Staff

Head teacher

The most important member of staff to meet and get to know is the head teacher. Their beliefs and ways of doing things will underpin how the school is organised and run. The things they believe are important will be highlighted and promoted. Always make sure you have met this member of staff before placing a child within the school.

As a parent, you must feel able to like and trust this person and to be able to talk to them if you have a concern or problem regarding your child. Look out for a head who appears:

- warm and welcoming to parents;
- proud of the school;
- confident that you will like what you see;
- competent;
- organised;
- sympathetic;
- easy to talk to;
- interested in your family;
- to have a rapport with children;
- to have a clear vision of what they want for the school;
- to know what they are talking about with regard to primary education;
- to have a high regard for their staff.

It is useful to watch the head interacting with the children and other members of staff as this will give you an insight into relationships within the environment.

Ratio of staff to children

How many members of teaching staff and support staff are there, and what is the typical ratio of adults to children in the infant/junior departments? Class size and adult-to-child ratio do have a direct impact on the amount of attention and support your child will receive in the classroom.

Turnover

Ask if there is or has been a high turnover of staff in the school – a high turnover is a bad sign. Children need continuity, and teachers leaving and starting on a regular basis can be disturbing and unsettling. It can also suggest that staff relationships are not good and the team is not working well together.

Teaching staff

Ideally, schools should have a mixture of experienced and less experienced teaching staff to complement one another – wisdom and experience mixed with new energy and new initiatives make for a good team. It is also good to have a gender mix in the staffroom, although most primary staffrooms are overwhelmingly female.

Keep your eyes open for teachers who are:

- genuinely interested and caring;
- calm and supportive;
- speaking to children in a respectful, non-patronising way;
- engaging the children in an interesting and stimulating way during whole-class teaching times;
- using a range of visual aids as well as talking to children if they are carrying out a whole-class lesson;
- asking the children questions and listening carefully to the answers;
- praising children regularly for their behaviour and work;
- walking and talking;
- scanning the classroom regularly to check children are on task;
- organised and competent;
- proud to show off their classroom and displays.

Meeting your child's future class teacher

If possible, it is important that you meet the teacher who will be having your child in their class and that you get a feel of his or her classroom. This will be the most important person in your child's life besides you for the first year in the school. Pay particular attention to what is going on in this teacher's classroom, as this will be the environment in which your child is to settle and, hopefully, thrive.

Special expertise of staff

Has the school got staff with expertise in a particular subject or field? On the whole, primary-school teaching staff are 'Jacks of all trades', but some have training and expertise in a specialist area, such as special needs, music, maths or art. This can make a great deal of difference in how this area is promoted within the school.

Support staff

Most schools will have a variety of support staff who help teachers in the classroom with children with special needs and with the everyday running of the class and preparation of materials. LEA schools also employ Midday Supervisors (known colloquially as 'dinner ladies') to supervise children during the dinner break. Check on the ratio of midday supervisors to children.

Environment

Distance

It is important to consider the time taken and ease of getting to the school and back. The journey will have to be undertaken rain or shine, twice a day, ten times a week, so it will become very much part of your life. Can you walk? Is the car journey fraught with traffic? How long will it take on a good or bad day? Is there a bus/train to get there? Is there a school bus, and is it going in the opposite direction to the one you take to work? Is it possible for the child-minder to fetch your child from it? These are all questions to bear in mind.

Location

Is the school in a quiet residential environment, or on a busy main road? A main road might mean constant fumes and noise pollution floating into the playground. What is the traffic like around the school at dropping off and collecting times? Is it impossible to park?

Condition of the school building

Research has indicated that pupils' educational success is partly linked to the structure, appearance and hygiene standards of the actual school building. Does the building appear run down with peeling paint, graffiti, or have a general aura of damp and decay, or is it well-maintained, bright and welcoming? Even large Victorian buildings well past their sell-by-date can be made more appealing and inviting through bright paintwork and good maintenance.

Security

What sort of security is there on the front entrance? Most schools now have security systems and visual camera eyes to monitor who is entering the school, nowadays, a very important precaution.

Lobby area

Is the entrance well sign-posted and the lobby area inviting and appealing? Good schools will have displays of children's work or photographs in the entrance area, which make a colourful and welcoming sight.

Outside buildings

If the school has several different buildings on site, how far do pupils have to go from the main school building to reach their classrooms? What is the state of these buildings – are they run down?

Size, space and light

Is the environment spacious and airy, or small and cramped? Do the classrooms appear completely crammed with children and furniture, or is there room for ease of movement? Is the building light, with plenty of windows? Buildings where the electric lights have to be on constantly can be a bit depressing.

Is the layout open-plan, or is each class very much its own entity with separate rooms along each corridor? Open layouts encourage teaching staff to work co-operatively and they enable children to have more space to spread out and work more independently. Individual classrooms can create a safe and cosy space that children relate to as their own.

Are there outside class spaces for practical activities such as painting or design?

Classroom environment

Is there a carpet area (particularly important for infants) where the teacher can conduct whole-class teaching? Has it got enough room for all the children to sit comfortably?

How are the tables and chairs arranged? In the infant school children usually sit in small table groups of four to eight so an adult can work with one small group at a time and the children can learn to work co-operatively together. This may continue in the junior school, although some schools now use a 'horseshoe' seating arrangement which many teachers feel is more conducive to good learning.

Are the walls covered with lots of varied examples of children's recent work – writing and artwork – mounted in a way which values their achievement? Are there display tables demonstrating practical activities or scientific experiments, or does everything look a bit faded and repetitive as though it has been around for months?

Does the classroom look well equipped with books and materials? Does it have a computer or computers?

Library

A well-stocked and comfortable library is a great asset to any school. It is important that there is a wide range of books to give children an opportunity to explore their interests at their particular reading ability.

Computer suites

All children need the opportunity to gain good computer skills and be part of the rapidly changing new technology which will shape their future. Some schools have set aside particular areas, sometimes in the library or a free classroom, to house fifteen or twenty computers where children can work as a group or class on IT activities.

Music rooms

Some schools will have support rooms such as a 'music room', especially when this subject area is something in which the school has a particular interest and expertise. This will be equipped with specialist materials and musical instruments to develop children's skill base. This may be something you are especially interested in if you have a musical family.

Sports hall/field/hardcore area

The facilities for sport can vary considerably within primary school provision depending on the space and grounds available and members of staff with the interest and ability to be able to coach youngsters. Some schools have a comprehensive list of after-school activities and set up matches with other teams. Others have very little team sports development and rely on physical education lessons to teach ball and passing skills. Most youngsters will not be ready to play team sports until they are seven or eight, so if this is something important to you, then it is best to explore just what is available.

School halls usually double up as school gyms and it is worth noting the range of climbing apparatus and equipment available.

Dining hall

In many schools, the school hall doubles up as a dining room *as well as* the school gym! In some rural village schools, where space is at a premium, the classroom itself becomes a dining room.

If your child is going to have school dinners, it is worth finding out who will be cooking them (many schools employ catering firms to bring meals on site) and what is a typical menu. If you have a 'fussy' eater, you may need to be reassured that someone will be making sure your child finishes his or her food. Does the school have a policy on table manners?

Outside area/playground

Do the infants have a separate play area to the juniors to avoid them being trampled underfoot or possibly picked on by older children?

Is the playground just a concrete back-yard, or is there a grass area or field for playing on when the weather is dry? Imagine the space filled with children or watch the children out at play for a while. Is there enough room for a wide range of play opportunities? Are there play-lines marked out for games such as hopscotch?

Is there any climbing apparatus to stimulate imagination and climbing games? Ask if the children have access to small-play equipment such as hoops, balls and bats or skipping ropes. Busy children are happy children. Is the playground divided into different areas so the footballers can play without kicking footballs into non-footballers' games? Is there a quiet area with seating for children to withdraw from the hubbub and chat with one another or sit in the summer to eat packed lunches?

Conclusion

Having completed your visits to various different schools you now have to make a choice. In the end, having taken all the above into account, it is our parental instincts that can be the most reliable indicator of the right school for our child. If we feel at home and welcome within a school, then our child will also. If we feel it is an exciting and stimulating environment, then so will our child. If you experience the staff as committed, dedicated professionals, that is probably what they are! Go with your gut feeling – that is why you are a parent; you know your child and you have the responsibility and the right to make judgements on behalf of him or her.

Having made a choice, you have made a commitment. That commitment is to support the school as a community and as the guardian of your child during school hours. You are now a parent in partnership with a school. In some senses, your responsibilities as a parent are now supported and shared by the school as an organisation and by teaching and non-teaching staff on a daily basis. In working together with them you create an environment that will allow your child to succeed and be happy.

3

The primary school child – understanding your child's development

In order to help our children to be successful in school it is extremely helpful to know the developmental stage they are at, and to understand the different sorts of ways they will be reacting and behaving during this time, both in the home and in the school environment. This chapter gives you a brief resumé of what you can expect in each year-group, although there are no hard or fast rules, as children will be slightly different in the way they develop and do things.

Reception class (4–5 years)

Children of four to five years old will be sociable human beings. They are beginning to choose their own friends and have an understanding of the need for rules and fair play. They enjoy playing with other children and understand taking turns. They can show concern for young children and siblings and sympathy for friends who fall over or are unhappy, and will try to comfort them. They enjoy dressing up and playing imaginative games both alone and with other children. They enjoy building things outside, such as dens, and inside, such as junk models. They love handling and playing with pets and can help to look after them in small ways.

The average four-to-five-year-old can be sensible and controlled and sit still for short periods of time, although this is very variable in the individual. They can be extremely strong-willed and defiant in their behaviour, and rude and truculent when things don't go their own way. They can also be moody and aggressive with both adults and children, but can be co-operative, sweet, loving and compliant too.

Their speech is becoming more clear and grammatically correct, and they are usually able to give their name, address and age without problems. They know when their birthday is and are very keen on the date arriving, and they will be asking continual questions, such as 'why?' 'when?' and 'how?', which can drive the average parent mad! They enjoy listening to stories and can follow a basic plot and have an understanding of character and motivation of people in the story. They enjoy finding out the meaning of different words and phrases and using them in everyday conversation.

They have an understanding of time and that different things happen at different times of the day and night. They have some appreciation of the concept of past, present and future, although this is not fully developed.

Children of this age can draw simple outlines of people or houses and count fingers on one hand with the index finger of the other. They can name some primary colours and match others. They can usually recognise their Christian name when written and will be trying to write their name themselves.

Physically, they are showing greater and greater competency in hand–eye co-ordination. They can run quite fast and are active and skilful in climbing, sliding, swinging, skipping and dancing. They are beginning to be able to catch and kick balls with accuracy and can climb ladders and trees and ride a tricycle. They are able to hit a ball with a large bat and direct it back towards a partner.

Emotionally, the four-to-five-year-old is extremely volatile. Happiness and delight can quickly change to temper tantrums or anxiety and tears, and back again. They may well have anxieties and fears that are expressed through nightmares or reluctance to go to school or stomach aches and feeling sick.

Children of this age are beginning to look after many of their needs independently, such as dressing and undressing. They will need only minimal support with things such as laces, buttons and ties. They will be able to wash and dry their face and hands, but may need help with the rest of bathing. They are able to use a knife and fork when eating, although may still need help cutting up tougher meat.

They are ready to take that step into independence by attending school and becoming their own individual person away from home.

Year 1 (5–6 years)

Year 1 children enjoy playing with other youngsters and are beginning to be able to play structured games without adult support. They are developing preferences for certain kinds of games and activities and will seek out other children who share their preference to play with. Six-year-olds are more aware of their own gender and will begin to choose toys and activities which identify them as a 'boy' or a 'girl'. They will also look more to their same-sex parent as a role model. Boys, in particular, enjoy doing things with their dads, and observing what it means to be male.

Five-to-six-year-olds are extremely active and like to set themselves physical challenges in the park or playground. They benefit from having plenty of opportunities to run around and let off steam. Children of this age are building on their physical competence and often learn to ride a two-wheeler bicycle and to swim. They are constantly fidgeting, and are up and down, busy with this and that.

Year 1 children are extremely curious and interested in the world around them. They prefer problem-solving through practical kinaesthetic activity rather than listening and absorbing information.

They are beginning to observe what others can do, and they want to compete. They often set themselves tasks which are beyond them, and then become frustrated and angry. Screaming fits and temper tantrums still belong to the six-year-old, although he/she is becoming aware that some places are more appropriate to have these fits than others; for example, they are totally unacceptable at school.

The average five-to-six-year-old is good at starting activities, but sometimes has trouble finishing them, or even getting halfway through, and will need adult encouragement and support. This is because concentration and attention span still need outside motivators rather than merely being internal disciplines. Children of this age have a poor attention span and often do not follow through tasks because they become absorbed in something else and forget or cannot hold the number of instructions given in their heads. They are better at doing tasks being helped by an adult rather than doing tasks on their own. Parents are more likely to get results by saying, 'let's put the toys away together' than by expecting the child to do it on their own.

At home, children benefit from a consistent and well-regulated schedule which gives them security and boundaries. Often, six-year-olds can show regressive, more babyish behaviour when they feel stressed, anxious, or out of control. This can involve going back to sucking their thumb or talking in a babyish way, or carrying around a comforter toy. This can be a signal to the parent to give more comfort, reassurance and attention. There is still a great need for physical closeness, hugs and cuddles.

Year 2 (6–7 years)

The Jesuits (an old Catholic order of teaching priests) once said: 'Give us a child until he is seven, and we will give you the man.' It is certainly true that a lot of our major personality and temperament characteristics are in place by the time we are seven.

Children are becoming more involved with their friendship groups and have a much better idea of what qualities to look for in a friendship. Boys tend to operate within a group, while girls may have established a small friendship bond with one or two other girls. Friendships can experience many ups and downs at this age. Children are able to play games with more complicated rules, and much of their imaginative play encircles themes about goodies and baddies, and role-play of known adults such as parents and teachers or popular film and television characters.

Year 2 children still find the concept of losing a game hard to tolerate. Often, if they appear to be losing a game, they will say they are bored and don't want to play any more.

If they do lose, they may tip the board over angrily. They are also quite capable of sly cheating in order to win, although they are gradually becoming aware of the concepts of fairness, skill and luck in playing games.

Children are beginning to calm down at this age and not be so volatile in their behaviour and mood. They are less likely to have screaming or temper tantrum fits and are beginning to be able to manage their anger and to control their feelings. This might become manifest in their becoming sullen and withdrawn when they are upset, which can be seen as an advance in control and an alternative to screaming and throwing themselves about. It might also include slamming doors or stomping about to show their disapproval when things don't go their way.

Children of this age still need reminders, guidance and firm boundaries from adults. They also need to know that they can make mistakes and be forgiven and start again with a clean slate. They are better able to respond to being talked to and given new strategies to manage their behaviour than being lectured or scolded in an angry or aggressive way. They appreciate, and are motivated by, praise and encouragement.

Children of this age have little sense of humour and cannot be cajoled through using humorous comments. They tend to think people are laughing *at* them rather than *with* them and will become upset and angry. They do not understand sarcasm, only that the tone of the adult is aggressive or angry, and they respond badly to it.

Year 2 children are capable of developing the skills that will allow them to play team games in the future, such as passing the ball, but still are not able to understand the concept that passing the ball may help the team as a whole. They are still keen to hold on to the ball themselves. Nevertheless, their physical competence at climbing, swinging, hopping, moving to music and running all rapidly improve and become smoother and more co-ordinated.

Most six-to-seven-year-olds can tell the time, have an understanding of the different seasons, and have a concept of a twelve-month year although they may not be able to fully recite all the months. They also have an internal sense of time which will alert them to what will happen next.

Year 3 (7–8 years)

Year 3 children are becoming less egocentric and more able to understand and empathise with the feelings of others, even people they don't know. Their friendship bonds are becoming stronger and they will enjoy having children to play at their house and going to visit other children's houses. They are beginning to understand that different people can have different expectations and ways of doing things and be able to adjust their own behaviour accordingly. Girls, particularly, can have big fallings out at this age and can be extremely unkind to one another and then best friends again the next day. This is a prime time for bullying behaviour to emerge in the classroom.

This is an age when children learn to concentrate for longer and more intense periods of time, screening out distractions and focusing on one thing. They do not like interruptions and sometimes can appear to be deaf when their parents call them to do something else. If your child does not respond to being asked to do something, it may not be because they are ignoring you but rather because their absorption in another task has made them unaware of your voice. You need to get their attention through touch or asking them to look at you before giving the instruction.

Many children develop high expectations of themselves and therefore become disappointed, frustrated or angry at their performance when it doesn't match their high ideals. They set themselves against classmates who seem to find particular skills easier than themselves. When this happens at school, children of this age can often act out their frustration at home by becoming rude and truculent towards a parent when they come out of school.

Seven- and eight-year-old children still have difficulties in articulating their feelings. The role of the parent is to try to encourage emotional literacy in children, giving them a language in which to verbalise the things that have gone wrong and to speak out their anger and frustration rather than lashing out. Sometimes, suggesting a range of options that the child might be feeling can allow the child to make a choice of the feeling that best describes what it is they are going through. Children of this age need to become aware that we cannot help our thoughts and feelings but we can choose or decide what to do about them.

Year 3 children are extremely interested in the concept of justice and fairness. A constant cry may be 'it's not fair'. Sadly, this is one of the things we have to learn in life – it isn't particularly fair, and not everyone has access to the same resources or giftings as others. This is a hard lesson for children to learn.

Seven- and eight-year-olds begin to be able to play team games and to be motivated by the concept of the group, sometimes putting aside their own needs and wants for the greater good of the group. This is a good time for them to join community youth teams.

They are also beginning to seek identity with others – who they are and what they enjoy playing – and to listen to or watch television. They begin to have outside heroes and heroines that they may seek to emulate like famous footballers or pop stars.

Year 4 (8–9 years)

The average eight-year-old can be very selfish and demanding at times, but also can show great consideration and kindness towards others. He or she is becoming more easy-going in mood and behaviour and is less likely to have dramatic outbursts of temper.

Children appear more settled at this age and more at home 'in their own skin', although they may sometimes become impatient with themselves or with others. They are extremely curious about everything and can be quite nosy, with 'big ears' listening into other people's conversations. They will have greater interest in what other people are thinking and feeling and be more ready to articulate their own feelings.

Children between the ages of eight and nine are capable of sustained activity within a group, and they enjoy the camaraderie of the group situation. They are able to lose at games and be disappointed but no longer cry or be upset. Nevertheless, children of this age are extremely sensitive to criticism, especially in front of others, and they are becoming much more self-conscious and aware of themselves.

This is a time when children become interested in their 'roots' and enjoy digging out the photograph album and looking at old pictures of themselves and asking questions about different members of the family. They love to hear stories about how they used to behave and can tolerate funny and amusing anecdotes about themselves. Children begin to plan a future for themselves and like to tell you what they are going to be when they grow up.

Eight- and nine-year-olds are fast developing a sense of humour. They enjoy riddles and lavatorial jokes that can drive a parent mad!

They begin to see things in a wider context and make assumptions and conclusions on the basis of their observations.

By this time, most children have acquired the basic skills of reading, writing and arithmetic and therefore have access to many more forms of communication that are not dependent on adult support. This opens up the world to them in a way that was not possible before.

Year 5 (9–10 years)

Year 5 children are becoming more responsible, co-operative and dependable. Mood swings are more unusual and therefore they appear more stable and happy. They can concentrate for much longer periods and with a greater intensity. The nine- and ten-year-old hopefully has established literacy skills and is able to express him or herself through a range of different mediums such as writing, music, art and drama.

Nine-year-olds have much greater planning and organisational skills and can be encouraged to get their own school bags and lunchbox ready. They also like to have a measure of independence, such as walking to the local shop to buy bread, or playing in the park with their friends. Nine-to-ten-year-olds are greater thinkers; they like to reflect on things and come to conclusions. They also like to classify, identify and order information. Often, they will start to collect something at this age or enjoy a particular hobby on a specific subject.

Peer pressures and demands are becoming increasingly evident at this age. Children begin to be more aware of what they look like and what they wear and will demand a certain kind of haircut, clothes and shoes. They will begin to notice what is perceived to be 'cool' or 'uncool', and will want to follow trends on television or in the media.

Children are used to working in a group and have learned to subordinate their needs to the group, therefore becoming much more adept in the team situation at achieving the best results. They become more interested in competitive sport and although they may not like to lose, they learn how to lose gracefully. They enjoy the social aspects of the game.

Children at this age may well become more 'allergic' to the opposite gender and tend to choose to both play and work at school in mostly same-sex groups. This tends to be a precursor to the beginnings of adolescence, with children learning the traits of their culture which define them as male and female.

Nine- and ten-year-olds can be trusted to follow through instructions and become more competent at everyday tasks such as making a cup of tea or a sandwich. They become more independent in their thinking and are beginning to develop their own views and opinions as opposed to those of the family group or parent.

Year 6 (10–11 years)

Children of this age are in the top class of primary school and feel very grown up. They can take on responsibilities at home and at school to carry out tasks and chores. They appear relaxed and casual for much of the time and can participate in discussions of social and world problems and give an opinion. This is a very good time for parents to talk about matters such as sex and relationships, drugs, alcohol and other subjects that may be more difficult to raise during adolescence when children are less likely to want to talk.

Friends are now in direct competition with the family for the ten-year-old's focus, time and sense of self-worth. Ten-year-olds will be listening to their peer group's views and opinions and can well choose these over the prevailing view of the family. Boys may fight, wrestle, shove and punch to show friendship, and sport becomes a focus for mutual interest and affiliation. Girls tend to hold hands, gossip, write notes and analyse friendships. Sharing secrets and wondering about the mysteries of the adult world are very typical of ten-to-eleven-year-olds.

Ten- and eleven-year-olds still enjoy family activities and get-togethers, but will also be beginning to organise their own social life and make their own arrangements to see friends. You may be surprised at the way they talk and relate to their friends as it seems very different from the way they talk and relate within the family unit.

There will be more focus on what to wear and how to look, and children will become increasingly self-conscious about their appearance. It is important for children to have the 'right' clothes and things, but they must accept that these have to be within the financial boundaries of the parental budget.

Children of this age hate to be shown up in front of their friends or told off in public so it is better to criticise and correct in private rather than in front of peers or other family members.

While it is important to recognise that children of this age are pre-adolescent and growing up, it is also vital to remember that they are still children who need love, attention, touch, praise and boundaries.

4

Home–school partnership

Starting school

When children start primary school, they face a big challenge: they step into a measure of independence as a unique individual without you by their side. They leave the familiar environment of the home, where there are people whom they know and love, to meet new adults and children, and they have a whole new building to find their way about. The way people behave and do things at school may be very different from the way things are done at home. Schools tend to be places of routine and structure where there are particular expectations: children will have to learn to sit still, listen, concentrate, pay attention and absorb information in line with school expectations. They will also be noticing themselves alongside their peer group and making comparisons in the way they perform and achieve.

For some children, going to school will be their first experience of being away from their parents. Others will already have been prepared by attending a playschool, nursery or childminder. While most children find going to school an enjoyable and stimulating experience, others find it an extremely daunting one. Changes and new things are always stressful even if they are positive. Children need plenty of support from home and their parents to make a good start in their new school.

Some children become anxious and nervous on separation at the school gate or classroom door, and can become tearful and upset. Some find it extremely difficult to conform to what is expected of them in the classroom and want to do their own thing without following the teacher's instruction. Some children find the demands for a new level of concentration, sitting still and listening overwhelming. Usually these problems gradually fade away as going to school becomes more habitual and normal and as the child adjusts to the new demands.

Young children find it difficult to articulate their fears, anxieties or difficulties in their new environment and you may find that your child regresses into more babyish behaviour at home or becomes more difficult or aggressive. This will usually settle down as the child becomes more settled at school.

As a parent, you can prepare your children for the experiences that school will bring them and make them more ready and adept to deal with their new measure of independence.

- Children's attendance at a pre-school setting is an excellent preparation for school life as it involves a short separation from parents or carers in the morning or afternoon and allows them to become used to the routines and structures of an institutional environment.
- If children don't attend a pre-school, then give them opportunities to separate from you and spend time with other adults such as grandparents, or do a 'swap' for a day and let your child play at a friend's house. This gives children the opportunity to feel confident about being without you for a few hours.
- Giving children lots of opportunities to play with other youngsters in the park or at home gives them a chance to develop social skills that will aid their ability to make friends and relationships and play positively with one another.
- Encouraging and helping your child to dress themselves independently is very important. Make sure that your child has a coat

that is easy to put on and take off, without a stiff zip or buttons, as this will most likely be put on and taken off throughout the school day. If possible, teach your child to tie shoelaces, be able do up shirt and trouser buttons, and tie their own school ties. If this proves a problem, then buy shoes that are done up with Velcro, and tie the tie, cut it at the back and put it on a bit of elastic so the child can put it on themselves over their heads. During PE activities, they will have to change into PE kit as quickly as possible. Although teachers and classroom assistants will help, there are probably about thirty children in the class so obviously this can be a time-consuming activity. Gym shoes with elastic fitting as opposed to trainers can be much easier to put on for a quick change.

- Make sure your child is confident in going to the toilet, wiping their bottom and washing their hands. The school staff do not expect to have to help children in these areas unless they have a special need.

- Teach your child how to use cutlery so they are able to eat their school dinners in a polite and acceptable way.

- Mark all your child's equipment with his or her name so if things are mislaid at school they can be found quickly.

The Home–School Day

As our children settle into school, there are a number of ways in which we can help them to be successful through what we do every day to both ease the home/school transfer, and provide a well-ordered routine and smooth running home environment for children. Here are some of the ways we can do this during the day:

Before school

- Wake your child in plenty of time to get up, get dressed and have breakfast without rushing and worrying about the time. If your child is a bit of a daydreamer, they may need more support in not becoming distracted and drifting off to play or watch TV before they are ready. It is a good idea to say that no TV or playing can happen until they are dressed for school and have had breakfast.

- Make sure your child has a good breakfast. Research indicates that children who have had a good breakfast are more alert, able to concentrate for longer periods of time, and better able to cope with their school work. Sitting down together with your child to have breakfast can help them to eat. Cereal, toast or some kind of protein such as egg or bacon will set your child up to make the most of their morning at school.

- Make sure that your child has a long drink before they go to school and include a bottle of water or fruit juice in their bag. Research shows that dehydration is a major cause of lack of attention and concentration, and the brain functions less well as the body dehydrates. It is important that children drink regularly.

- Leave for school in plenty of time so there is no rush and therefore no anxiety or apprehension. When children are late for school, they miss out on the beginning of the day and often on the explanations for the first task of the day. It will take them longer to settle down and understand what to do. It also means they may have to walk into a room of children who are already settled and organised, which is difficult and sometimes causes a great deal of stress.

- Have a board in the kitchen or by the front door to remind yourself of anything special that your child has to bring into school.

- If your child has a packed lunch, then make sure you make a healthy meal which has a mixture of mainly carbohydrate and protein and some fat to give maximum energy to revitalise your child in the middle of what is a long day. Don't give them a huge amount (the same amount as you might eat), as this can be overwhelming and mean they can't face eating any of it. Try to include some fruit as well as a chocolate or cereal bar treat. Make sure they have plenty to drink, water as well as fruit juice.

- Make sure that your child is dressed in a way which will keep them warm, cool or dry as the weather demands.
- If possible, try to have a five-minute sit down with your child before leaving the house, perhaps watching TV or reading a book, or having them reading to you to calm them down, and have a cuddle before the beginning of the school day.
- Walk to school if possible. A walk at the beginning of the day can help children to absorb their early morning energy and arrive at school having had some fresh air and exercise and ready to sit down to work. It is quite good for parents too! It also avoids cluttering up school streets with too many cars proving a danger to children.

End of the school day

- Be on time to fetch your child or make sure that whoever is fetching them has a commitment to be on time. Most children coming out of school scan the horizon for a friendly and known face and can become anxious if you or their arranged carer are not there. Some children have a fear of being left behind or abandoned and become worried if you are late. If you *are* unavoidably late it is worth ringing the school and warning them so that they can inform your child and make sure he or she is looked after until you get there.
- Bring a snack of a carton of fruit juice and a cereal or chocolate bar with you to the school gates. Often children have very low blood sugar when they emerge from school, having used up huge amounts of energy during the school day. This can cause them to be moody, stroppy and difficult when they leave the school gates. A little snack can raise blood sugar levels and avoid these problems and rows breaking out in the car or along the street.
- Recognise that children are tired after the school day and need time to veg out and relax. They need to be given the opportunity to play and choose their own activities after the more structured and compliant way they have been behaving at school. They

also need your attention. It is best to sit down with your children or be prepared to spend some time playing with them rather than become immediately overwhelmed by household chores.

- Homework teaches children how to work independently and to develop the habit of doing some learning outside the confines of the classroom. However, it can also become a big source of stress and battle between parents and children. Often, children feel that the last thing they want to do after a long day at school is to settle down and do another learning task.

Homework for younger children usually consists of reading their reading book and possibly learning a few spellings. As children go up into the Juniors, they may be expected to do twenty to thirty minutes on other subject areas. This is to prepare them for secondary education where they will have to do several homework subject areas every evening.

Homework is best tackled in a number of ways. First, set a specific time for it to be done. This will depend on your child and your afternoon/evening routine. Some children like to do their homework straight away when they get home to get it out of the way and know that the rest of the evening is free. Other children like to completely relax, watch their favourite TV and have a play and then sit down to their homework. It is best not to leave it too late otherwise your child will be too tired to concentrate. However, if the routine is that homework is always done at, say, six o'clock, then children are far more likely to settle down.

Choose an appropriate place to do it. Reading together can be done sitting on the sofa, but if there is written homework, then children will need a table and chair and good lighting. The kitchen table is ideal because you can sit with them, perhaps engaged in another task but ready to help if necessary. Children will respond to how you prioritise and view their homework. By being prepared to sit down with them and help and support them, you are showing that you value them and their school work and that you think it is important and worth doing.

One of the purposes of homework is that children learn to work independently, so how much help should you give them as a parent? Remember to support rather than actually do the homework! This can involve merely sitting with them or helping with finding information, spellings, and encouraging them to problem-solve a question. If the homework seems to be too challenging for your child, and you really think they have been set a task that is too difficult for them, then it is important to talk to the teacher.

- When children are at school, they need a firm bedtime routine that will ensure they calm down and get off to sleep at a reasonable time. Going to school is a tiring business and they need proper rest and sleep to be able to cope with the following day. Again, structure and routine are the best ways to achieve this.

Choose a time to start the bedtime routine, one that will be the same every day so children know that this is the time they will start getting ready for bed. If your child is absorbed in playing or watching something, warn them ten minutes and then again, five minutes, before this time that it is nearly time to get ready for bed. Often, children become annoyed and irritable if they are asked to stop an activity in mid-flow – just like we would!

A bath and/or changing into pyjamas signals the wind-down to the end of the day. This is an opportunity to talk and listen to your child and maybe hear more about what happened at school that day. It is a time when you can curl up with a good book together and share a story or two. Your child may then be ready to go to sleep. If not, they can play or look at books for an agreed period of time before the light is turned off.

We are all creatures of habit and the more we stick to our set routine, the more chance we have that our child will be compliant and accept that routine. Children cannot be at their best at school if they haven't had a good night's sleep, and it is essential that we as parents make sure that everything is in place to allow this to happen.

- In order to ensure things run smoothly in the morning, it is good to have your child's clothes and uniform laid out the night before, ready to put on without a fuss. School bags can be packed with all that is necessary for the next day and put by the front door so there isn't a panic in the morning with something missing and having to be found!

Being a parent schools appreciate

Schools really do appreciate any help that parents can give them. This can be through helping children read, doing simple, practical, supportive tasks in the classroom, or helping to fund-raise for the school coffers. Or perhaps by becoming a parent governor, helping debate major decisions in running the school, or being involved in the Parent Teacher Association (PTA), organising events such as Christmas fairs, school barbecues or discos. It could be volunteering to help take children swimming or on school trips when extra adults are always needed.

If you are not able to do any of the above due to work or other commitments, there are still some basic things you can do to make the school appreciate your input as a school parent working in partnership with them:

- Check your child's school bag for notes or letters. Reply as quickly as possible to any requests.
- Attend parents' evenings to get feedback on your child's development.
- Keep your child's class teacher informed if there are any major stresses and strains in your child's life so they can show understanding in the classroom.
- If there are any problems or difficulties, work in partnership with the school to overcome them – avoid becoming aggressive or defensive as emotional outbursts rarely help the situation.
- Attend school functions and PTA events and support them with your presence and money.
- Be appreciative to members of staff who are looking after your

child and helping to educate them – if your child has made any complimentary comment, then pass it on! We all need praise and encouragement.

- Ring first thing if your child is off sick and tell the school. Give a note to the school office explaining what was wrong when your child returns to school.
- If your child has school dinners, make sure that they take the money in on Mondays.
- Check that your child has everything needed for school every morning.
- Be on time – both in the morning when arriving at school, and in the afternoon, when fetching your child.
- If there is a home/school or home reading report book, write in it, giving the teacher some feedback on how your child has got on at home.
- Make sure your child has completed their homework – help with reading and spellings.
- Show an interest in what is going on in the classroom – go in sometimes and remark on some of the displays on the wall – teachers need appreciation too!
- Show support at school sports matches or the school sports day, or in coming to class assemblies or school plays – your child needs to see your face in the crowd!
- Try to avoid taking your child out of school for occasional days or for long holidays – this means the teacher will have to spend some time making sure they catch up and it will cause problems for your child.

The key development skills

If we want our children to succeed at school, we have to see ourselves as working in partnership with schools to help develop key learning, social and behavioural skills. It is this essential partnership that creates the fertile ground in which a child can grow.

Schools are focusing on a range of skill development that needs to be reflected in our parenting and the kind of activities, stimulation and emotional support we are giving our children at home.

Primary schools are required, first of all, to prioritise the learning of the basic literacy and number skills. They must try to ensure all children can read and write independently and confidently and that they have acquired a range of important mathematical concepts by the time they reach eleven.

The National Curriculum also involves primary schools in the teaching and setting up of learning experiences for children that will ensure they have access to a wide range of different subject bases and skill areas, including subjects such as history, geography, science, music, art, drama, religious education and physical education.

Perhaps, most importantly of all, they are also intrinsically involved in the social, emotional, spiritual and behavioural development of your child.

There are some areas of child development and learning that run like threads through the fabric of every primary school setting. These all interact with the natural learning happening within your home environment, and they are all areas that you can support and assist your child in developing. They are:

- development of social skills;
- development of behavioural skills;
- development of language skills – speaking and listening;
- development of concentration and attention skills;
- development of reading skills;
- development of writing skills;
- development of mathematical skills;
- development of scientific understanding;
- development of an understanding of the notion of 'past' and gaining an historical perception on how people lived long ago;
- development of geographical knowledge and understanding of the world;

- development of design and technological skills;
- development of competency in information and communication technology;
- development of musical awareness and musical composition;
- development of creativity and artistic expression;
- development of physical competence and co-ordination;
- development of spiritual awareness and religious knowledge;
- development of personal, social and health education and of citizenship.

All these skills are skills that we as parents can support, encourage and stimulate. We may also need to take a key role if we wish our child to be successful within the school environment. In the next few chapters we will look at how these skills are being developed in primary school and how we can develop them at home.

5

Development of social skills

Developing good social skills is an extremely important part of growing up and learning to deal with other people. Human beings are basically social creatures: all day and every day we are meeting all kinds of different people whom we need to relate to, communicate with, and talk and listen to. Sometimes, these interactions will be brief civil exchanges, at other times, there will be more complex emotional interchanges with family and friends. Relationships are built on good social skills and a level of 'emotional literacy', i.e. the ability to read other people's body language and facial expressions, to understand and empathise with other people's feelings, and to be able to express and articulate our own feelings. Good social skills will carry us through life – people with good social skills are more likely to be happy, in employment, and have long-lasting relationships.

Good social skills will ensure your child's popularity and successful interaction both in school and in later life. Children of four or five will already have an incredible awareness of social situations, appropriate and inappropriate behaviour, and 'how to win friends and influence people'! However, some children, who have not had much experience of playing with other children, or who are shy and less outgoing, will find social interaction an overwhelming process. Going to school provides a further learning opportunity for all children to develop their social skills. We can complement this learning by talking to children about their social experiences and by helping them through the process of new relationships.

School partnership

School is a socially interactive environment. Most children have twenty-nine other people to get along with in their class alone, not to mention all the children they come across in the playground. Schools encourage and promote social development as essential to community living.

Children need to learn to respect other children's needs and feelings and to be able to share and co-operate with others. They must learn to take turns when playing with games and with equipment. It is important for the child to understand that someone else may have a different point of view from themselves and that this is not only acceptable but has to be tolerated. Children need to develop a real understanding and empathy with other people's feelings. This involves being aware of their own feelings and being able to describe them so they can articulate their own needs and consequently also be able to put themselves in someone else's shoes. Children also have to learn to manage the frustration that comes when people do not do what they want!

In the infant school there will probably be a 'home corner' where children can exercise their imaginations and role-play co-operatively with one another. The school will provide simple board games and a range of toys the children can play with such as a train set, car track, farm, dolls house or construction toys. Children move from playing alongside one another to playing together, they learn to take turns, and this is a natural part of their development.

Children in school are constantly being given opportunities to work at tasks together and to share ideas. Staff will work with small groups of children on a shared activity to encourage and promote this sharing of ideas and task completion. As children get older, they will be encouraged to work co-operatively in table groups discussing ideas. They will often have the opportunity to work in pairs to carry out research or complete a task. This might involve working on a computer or planning a piece of work together.

Many schools have developed a technique called 'Circle Time' when a whole group of children sit in a circle sharing thoughts and feelings regarding a particular topic. For example: I feel happy when . . .' or 'I feel sad when . . .' Children learn that we all share a range of reactions and feelings to the same kinds of situations. They also have an opportunity to be listened to, and this raises their self-esteem and a belief that they do have important things to say.

On the sports field, older children will begin to learn to play team games. They start to realise that victory lies in the co-operation of the whole team rather than the skill of the individual player. If a goal is to be scored, then the ball must be passed rather than held by one person.

The school playground is a place where children can really suffer if they have poor social skills. A reluctance or inability to play with other youngsters can mean isolation and loneliness. Some children will become very frustrated and physically aggressive because they have not learned to control their impulses when others upset them or don't do what they want them to do. Children who are successful at friendships are co-operative, supportive, and able not only to articulate their own needs, but to understand others' needs. They are usually full of ideas or able to take up other people's ideas. They have a strong concept of interaction and engagement.

Schools should support children who are struggling with social interactions and see it as a lack of skill rather than children being introverted or badly behaved. Children can learn to interact more effectively, even if it doesn't come very naturally to them in the first place. Sometimes, children need to practise strategies to enable them to join in games, or have some gentle feedback on their bossiness or physical aggression which makes their peer group not want to play.

Good schools will set up good playground practice to encourage children to play successfully with one another. This might include having a wide range of objects such as balls, hoops, skipping ropes and bats which children can play games with. Some schools offer training to midday supervisors to be 'play leaders' helping children to develop constructive games and keep to the rules. Some develop 'quiet areas' where children can read, play games or chat, to accommodate children who are not so keen on rushing around constantly.

Some schools will have a 'can't say, won't play' rule, or have a bench in the playground where children who want to play with someone can sit and a little supportive group of older children will pick them up and start a game. This can encourage children to notice if someone is isolated or left out, and to empathise with how that might feel. The school can encourage an ethos of good social interaction.

Home partnership

We encourage our children's social skills by putting them in social situations. They can get a sense of the social world by attending family events and spending time with people of different ages and at stages of life. Grandparents can play a vital role in encouraging social skills as they often have the time and attention that young children need, and they can support parenting discipline in a gentle but effective way. Social behaviour is often learned around the dining table when children see adults and young people talking and interacting over a meal. We can teach our children to have a ready smile and good eye contact with people they meet. We can give them confidence to speak up and out when adults engage them in conversation.

Children also need other children to develop their social skills. Inviting a friend back to the house can be a huge learning curve for your child. They have to learn to accommodate a guest in their own environment and to share their toys and space. Now that children do not play out so much in the street environment due to fears for their safety because of traffic and stranger danger, it has increasingly become the role of parents to provide opportunities when they can mix with groups of children outside school. This can be at extra activities such as gymnastics or dance, or through belonging to a sports club. We can also take them to parks and sports fields to run around and meet other youngsters.

Often, there will be rows and fallouts when children are playing together. This is a normal part of growing up as young people learn to interact, negotiate and co-operate. Children learn that if they try to be too bossy and controlling, people won't want to play with them. Equally, they learn that getting angry or frustrated because the game is not going their way will mean the game usually ends in disaster. Children learn that there are consequences to their behaviour in social situations. They learn that in order to get on with other people we have to make ourselves agreeable, and sometimes modify our behaviour.

As parents, we can encourage our children's social confidence through our love and attitude towards them. If a child feels good about themselves, who they are and what they can achieve, then they are able to take the risks necessary to reach out to others and to communicate in a way which solidifies and builds relationships. Children who have poor self-worth can have difficulties managing their social behaviour, and can distrust others, therefore finding it difficult to make friendships or sustain relationships.

We can help our children to feel good about themselves through first of all appreciating them for who they are rather than having unreal expectations about how we would like them to be. Often, we carry our own baggage into the parenting process and seek either to fulfil our own ambitions or longings through our children or to have expectations that our children will never be able to achieve in a certain area because we were not able to as children either. Try not to force a square-shaped child into a round-shaped hole. Even within families, we can easily label children 'the sporty one', 'the clever one' etc. However, each of us is more a mosaic of different gifts and talents that make us up to be the unique person we are. Let your children grow in their own unique way and support that process as a supporter on the sidelines of the playing field rather than as a coach directing the game.

We need to recognise and respect our children's feelings and to give them an opportunity to express them, even if they are sometimes not what we want to hear. The most important aspects of social interaction include a level of emotional literacy. That is an ability to communicate our feelings and emotions to other people in a way in which they can understand. If we don't listen to our children, we will not give them the opportunity to develop this emotional literacy. We also need to express our own feelings to our children taking responsibility for them by using the words 'I feel' rather than 'you make me feel'. This models good emotional interaction for our children, and thus we all take responsibility for our own feelings and reactions to life rather than blaming others for making us angry.

Children sometimes do not have the necessary vocabulary to identify the name behind their feeling. They may not know the word 'jealousy' or be able to name the confusion of rage and temper as anger. We can help by making suggestions to our children such as 'it sounds like you are feeling very angry with Dan'. When children's feelings are acknowledged and accepted, and when they are not told that they are wrong to feel them, then they can learn to exercise the necessary self-control to contain them.

If our children are to be successful in a social context, they have to learn the parameters of that social context. It is OK to feel angry, but not to hit people because you are angry. It is OK to want to play the game your way, but if no one else wants to play it that way, you may have to compromise. It is OK to feel disappointed, but not OK to throw things around because you are disappointed.

Our children will need help when social situations get out of hand or when they are rejected, angry or sad. The world is not a perfect place and other human beings can let us down and cause us pain. We can be there to support our children through these times by allowing them to express their feelings, and through giving them strategies to deal with people who have upset them or hurt them. Children's friendships can be very up and down. There can be bullying, unkindness, bossiness, manipulation and rejection. However, children can also show extreme generosity, forgiveness, kindness and friendship – all in the same hour or day! This is all part of the process of growing up and learning to adapt to the social world. As parents, we can help our children's sense of self-worth to remain intact by continuing to love our children unconditionally and by being there, talking about it, and giving them practical strategies that our own experience has shown to work.

6

Development of behavioural skills

Behavioural skills are closely linked to social skills because they allow our children to become morally aware and to grow into respected, and respectful members of the community who behave in a socially acceptable way. Behavioural skills are also the bedrock of effective learning skills. Without good behavioural skills children will not be in a position to concentrate, listen, interact and absorb new information and learning. It is therefore essential that parents and schools work in partnership to teach and develop good behavioural skills. The more consistency there is in approach the more likely it is that children will feel secure and happy.

The framework for good behaviour both at home and at school can be outlined as consisting of:

- clear expectations – defining how we want children to behave;
- praise and rewards – encouragement works better than punishment;
- boundary setting – clear, consistent consequences for poor behaviour;

- good relationships – building children's self-esteem and self-worth;
- structure and routine – supporting habitual good behaviour;
- prioritising what is and isn't worth having a drama about – knowing when to ignore behaviour;
- keeping calm when others aren't – managing angry feelings when children step out of line;
- listening and talking – communication is a baseline for understanding why inappropriate behaviour is occurring and for developing strategies for doing something different;
- negotiation – giving children incentives and goals worth working towards;
- modelling behavioural skills – behaving in the way in which we want children to behave;
- teaching behavioural skills – teaching means communicating in a way in which children can understand a concept and learn it. They need to understand the reason behind it.

School partnership –
whole-school behaviour policy

As mentioned in chapter 2, the reputation and well-being of a school rests on its ability to promote positive behaviour within the school community. A good school will pay particular attention to its behaviour policy and how it promotes good behaviour throughout the school day. It will aim to raise the self-esteem of its pupils and have high standards of morality and discipline. Schools should be in the business of teaching children that with rights come responsibilities:

- If we have a right to be treated with respect then we have a responsibility to treat others with respect.
- If we have a right to learn then we have a responsibility to allow others to learn.
- If we have a right to education then we have a responsibility to engage in the educational process.

Expectations

The good school lays out its expectations of behaviour and the rights and responsibilities of community members. These are usually based on several types of expectations or rules.

Overall philosophy

The first set of expectations has to include those that cover the wider issues of morality: respect, right and wrong and responsibility. These outline the underlying philosophy of the school and often include inclusive statements that seek to create respect for all. For example, 'At St Mary's school we respect and want the best for everyone in the community.'

Community rules

Another set of expectations will cover the more mundane aspects of school life, ensuring health and safety and covering environmental issues. They instruct on daily routines, dress, movement round the school, and what may or may not be brought on to school premises. For example, 'Trainers are only to be worn in the gym and outside area', 'Walk on the left-hand side of the corridor', or 'Chewing gum is not to be brought into school.'

Classroom rules

These are rules that are in place for the duration of every lesson or session and which inform pupils of basic behavioural expectations – so teachers can teach and pupils can learn. They are the 'baseline' of skills children need to acquire in order to be able to learn effectively and gain from their education.

Classroom rules usually cover the following areas:

- co-operation – following instructions, doing as you are told;
- social behaviour – relating well to others, not disturbing others while working;
- readiness for learning – having the right equipment, arriving on time for lessons;
- listening skills – listening to the teacher and other students;

- seating in class – sitting still and not moving around the classroom inappropriately;
- equipment – looking after school property and using it for the right purpose.

Rewards and incentives

The most successful schools have a wide range of rewards and incentives to encourage and motivate children to keep the rules, behave well and work hard. Some people argue that children should not be rewarded for something they should be doing anyway. The outside world would argue otherwise – we know that motivators and incentives are more likely to get people working and succeeding. If people acknowledge we are doing well and praise and encourage us, then we are more likely to want to do the same again. Praise and encouragement build self-esteem and a sense of value in the individual – these are as necessary to children and young people as water to growing plants.

Good schools will offer a range of different rewards and incentives; the first and most important being plenty of verbal praise. Teachers who manage behaviour very successfully within the classroom use positive statements far more frequently than negative ones. Teachers who praise pupils who are behaving appropriately are more likely to reinforce this appropriate behaviour in the whole class. Teachers who notice and comment on inappropriate behaviour are more likely to reinforce the attention-giving potential of poor behaviour.

Good schools will make sure that all youngsters have access to a reward system and not just the high flyers or disruptive children who are being encouraged to behave better. Children who work hard and are always polite, helpful and kind should be held up as an example and rewarded accordingly.

Children's top reward is their parents knowing about their good behaviour so it is worth asking how you will know your child has behaved well and the school is pleased with them.

Other reward systems that reinforce verbal praise might include:

- *Class incentive schemes*
  This involves pupils earning points towards a whole class treat – pupils can earn points individually, or as a group or class. Peer pressure is towards obtaining the class treat and therefore eliminates the 'teacher creep' mentality. Treats could involve extra break time, watching a short video, playing a quiz, etc. Some primary schools have a special 'choosing time' known as Golden Time in order to reward good behaviour.

- *Star charts*
  These are a familiar sight in the primary school and enable children to put a star on a chart when they have behaved well or worked hard. These can accumulate to gain a prize or certificate.

- *Stickers*
  Stickers have great visual appeal and a child wearing one usually gets extra praise from other members of staff for their achievement.

Sanctions or consequences for bad behaviour

Children have a great sense of fairness and justice and like to see these exercised in school. Children appreciate firm boundaries that make them feel secure and safe and know that law and order are in place. How many of us would say that one of the characteristics of our favourite teacher at school was that they were 'firm but fair'?

Sanctions are not primarily about punishment. They are the boundaries put in place to warn children of their inappropriate behaviour and wrong choices. The aim of boundaries is to make the child consider the choice they are making and to weigh up the consequences of continuing that behaviour. Their ultimate aim is to enable that child to return to the appropriate behaviour. It is not the severity of a punishment that impacts on the child, but the consistency of delivery.

Good schools develop children's behavioural skills, self-discipline and control by making it clear that there will be clear foreseeable consequences to poor behaviour. This is in the same way that adults caught speeding when driving at over seventy miles an hour can expect to lose three points on their licence if stopped by the police. Schools can make this principle clear through a structured system of consequences (or punishments) enabling all members of staff to operate it consistently and effectively. It outlines how staff can be 'firm but fair' and provides a procedural framework for teachers to follow while keeping calm and collected.

The behaviour policy should outline the kind of consequences carried out within the school if children misbehave. You should be looking for:

- a system that appears fair, consistent and appropriate in response to the kind of inappropriate behaviour shown;
- all members of staff being committed to using the same system;
- consequences to be structured on an escalating scale according to the behaviour;
- the use of a warning system before a child is punished, that indicates the pupil has the choice to change his/her behaviour;
- a 'clean slate' policy once the consequence has happened, with the child able to start again in the next session or on the following day.

Staff modelling

One of the ways in which children learn positive behaviour is through watching adults. Staff who are respectful towards one another and towards children, will engender this behaviour in their classroom. Shouting, sarcasm and bullying tactics in teachers will also be reflected in the classroom or playground. Management who appreciate, praise and reward their staff for commitment and dedication will engender a working environment where youngsters are likely to do the same.

Pastoral care

Beyond the school behaviour policy, good schools will have an understanding of the emotional and behavioural difficulties of some youngsters. Many factors can affect the way in which children behave and relate to others and, without this understanding, schools cannot seek to help the young people in their care.

Parents can help schools by letting them know if there are any issues such as bereavement, separation, divorce, or economic factors which might be creating stress within the family. They can then make allowances for the child and give them extra attention and support.

Home-behaviour policy

Managing behaviour is one of the essentials of the 'good enough' parent and it is one of the most challenging tasks we will have to face. However, if we want our children to succeed both at school and in life, it is one that we will have to tackle. For our children to be accepted socially, for them to be liked and appreciated and for them to be able to concentrate and learn, they will need to be able to behave properly. If our children are not disciplined and can't behave, we will set them up to fail – at a basic level, people will not like their behaviour and therefore will avoid playing with them or inviting them round. They will also be unable to gain from and engage in the process of education.

It is a parental responsibility and duty to keep control of our children and to train them in socially acceptable behaviour. However, this is often easier said than done. Society has changed considerably over the last twenty-five years and the whole structure and hierarchy of authority and discipline has altered. Where there used to be automatic respect for elders, teachers and those in positions of authority in society, such as the police force or the church, this is no longer so. Now, we expect people to earn our respect and be somehow worthy of it. It is easy for 'authority' to 'slip from grace' as certain parts of the media tend to hound and undermine those in authority roles, given the slightest opportunity or failing. In the same way, it seems that parental authority, the underlying fabric of society, has in some ways been eroded in the minds of parents, the public and children. The disciplining of children is now increasingly perceived as the role of parents and parents alone rather than something the whole community shares a responsibility in. In the past, people in the community would feel free to step in and chastise a child if they were behaving in an unacceptable way. Now, we might be arrested for telling off someone else's offspring! So, although the responsibility and burden of parenting now falls squarely on parental shoulders, parental confidence seems to have hit an all-time low.

Many parents find it difficult to recognise their own authority. They may not fully appreciate that children require expectations and boundaries and the imposition of a certain amount of control in order to develop their own internal self-control and self-discipline in the future. In order for children to feel safe, loved and secure, they need boundaries – an imaginary, but firmly drawn, line that, when crossed, will mean there are consequences to their behaviour. However, how do we create these boundaries and controls to raise stable, well-adjusted adults?

While past generations may have used extremely controlling and aggressive methods of disciplining their children, since the sixties parents have sought other ways to raise children. Where beatings, smacking, shouting and punishment were the order of the day for unruly youngsters, we now seek a different pathway. This generation, and the one before it, have sought to give children rights and to make them accept responsibilities through negotiation, compromise and empowerment. The Children's Act 1989 has actually put these new rights for children into a legal framework that protects them and outlines their entitlements from society.

However, the new pathway of communication, negotiation and compromise has proved a difficult path for some parents to cope with. While many parents try their best to avoid smacking and shouting, they don't really know what to do instead. They are offered little training, sometimes judgement, disapproval and lack of support. Meanwhile, schools are experiencing more and more children with emotional and behavioural difficulties, children exhibiting anti-social and violent behaviour. These children seem to have few if any boundaries to their behaviour. They also appear to be inherently unhappy.

Is something going wrong? How can we as parents steer a path through discipline which is not aggressive, controlling or punitive, but is an extension of our legitimate love, care and regard for the well-being of our children? How can we bring about our long-term plan of raising children to be responsible, law-abiding, socially acceptable adults?

What we need is a near mirror reflection of what modern day schools do as organisations and what good teachers do as individuals. Just as there has been a big turn around in disciplinary methods within schools, so there needs to be a development in the way we discipline within the home. We all need a 'home-behaviour policy'. It is a policy or plan to achieve our goal: disciplined children who will grow into self-disciplined adults.

The first thing to remember is that our 'home-behaviour policy' must be a plan to raise children effectively. Something we create in the best future interests of our children, and not to control them or to confine them. Discipline is part of love, care and compassion for our children, not an obstacle to crush their spirit. Good discipline takes place when we operate within an environment of love, encouragement, praise, acceptance, tolerance and forgiveness (there is a lot of forgiveness necessary in the average family!).

Expectations

Like schools, parents must consider several different sets of expectations or rules within the home environment. All families are different and consequently will have a variety and range of different expectations. Perhaps on the smaller, less important issues, what may be acceptable in one family will not be in another. However, as a culture, we hopefully share some underlying common morality and values which are reflected in how we teach and train our children. If we are to raise law-abiding, respectful and respected adults, then our non-negotiable boundaries will be similar. These non-negotiable areas of behaviour in reality form the basis of all law, order and peace within a society. They form the baseline of the development of conscience in the growing child that will allow them to make moral judgements in the future.

Non-negotiable types of behaviour

What is the moral framework, what are the non-negotiable rights and wrongs of a home environment? These are the types of behaviour we are prepared to take a firm and consistent stance on. Areas where, as parents, we will not be moved and we will not compromise. These are issues regarding which we are prepared to 'lay down the law'. In our eyes, they are not matters to be met with negotiation or compromise. If children fail to abide by them, we will let them know in no uncertain terms what we feel, and will be likely to impose consequences.

These are some examples of non-negotiable behaviour:

- physically hurting other people;
- being cruel to, or hurting, animals;
- deliberate disobedience of a direct parental instruction;
- bullying behaviour;
- damaging or destroying property;
- stealing;
- swearing abusively;
- being rude to adults.

These kinds of behaviour will certainly not be acceptable in school or in the wider community. Children need to know the consequences of these kinds of behaviour. Ultimately, they may be excluded from school and lose their right to education. They will definitely experience a great deal of negative attention and rejection from the community. If we fail to curb such behaviour if and when it happens, we are responsible for our children's failure to meet society's expectations. We have let them down.

As parents, our response to a demonstration of such behaviour should be legitimate, controlled anger, disappointment, and a clear outline of our future expectations. We might initially show this through a raised voice, direct eye contact and assertive (as opposed to aggressive), body language. If a child has behaved in one of the above ways, he or she needs to realise that this is totally unacceptable to you and you will not tolerate it. It is legitimate for a child to feel ashamed but not humiliated. In order for a moral conscience to develop, shame for totally unacceptable behaviour or lack of respect towards others is legitimate. This might lead on to a discussion about what happened, what they were feeling at the time, and different choices they could make in the future. In doing this, we are protecting our children's acceptability in future society.

Negotiable types of behaviour

What are the types of behaviour we see as negotiable? This kind of behaviour can be regarded as part and parcel of childhood. It usually changes and fades as children are steered and guided by their parents into more acceptable forms of behaviour. This type of behaviour is important, and will change dependent on the age and stage of the child. However, such behaviour does not come into the same area of urgency as non-negotiable behaviour. It would include:

- children doing as they are told, e.g. brushing their teeth, within a reasonable time span;
- sharing toys;
- siblings playing together;
- good manners;
- doing chores;
- getting ready for school on time;

- controlling temper;
- eating healthily;
- limiting television watching;
- going to bed and to sleep without making a fuss;
- tidying up.

We should encourage these types of behaviour by praising children or giving them positive attention when they get it right. They should not become great battlefields in which the warriors (parent and child) have to fight to the end. There is room for negotiation or compromise. There is room for extra rewards – maybe a star chart to encourage the behaviour you want. Children naturally want to please their parents if they are given the encouragement to do so.

When children step out of line on these issues (as they will inevitably do), boundaries should be in line with the severity of the offence and could involve time out, the removal of privileges such as pocket money, television watching or time with friends.

'Let it go' behaviour

There are some types of behaviour that, as a parent, you may choose to ignore because it doesn't seem worth making a fuss or creating a drama. If we did not do this occasionally as parents, we might be driven totally crazy! These might include:

- putting feet on sofa (buy a throw);
- sibling bickering;
- whinging and whining;
- picking at food;
- levels of tidiness.

The tolerance for these will be different in different families. What I would let go would probably drive you insane, and vice versa!

It is incredibly helpful for you to sit down and work out your non-negotiable, negotiable and 'let it go' behaviour. This can define your home-behaviour policy and help you to set guidelines and boundaries that work for you as a family. Always remember that praise and encouragement for getting it right work best of all.

Good behaviour also comes from our building relationships with our children and operating in ways that encourage and motivate them to grow into responsible, emotionally stable, respectful, law-abiding and happy adults.

These are some of the ways we can do this:

- Notice your child's good behaviour – catch them being good.
  This gives the message that good behaviour gains approval, attention and praise. This makes it worth doing again as far as the child is concerned.
- Listen to children.
  Try to provide opportunities for each child to get a special spot each day when they can be on their own with you for just a few minutes – just before bedtime can be a good slot. Don't ignore children when they are trying to tell you something. If you can't talk about it at that moment then say, 'I can't talk about it now because I have to do this, but we can sit and talk about it at tea time and then I will really have time to listen to you properly.'
- Give children the opportunity to express their feelings (even if they are angry ones).
  Children need to learn to articulate and vocalise their feelings in order to develop emotional literacy and relationships with other people.
- Give clear messages by making simple, direct requests that are short and to the point.
  Don't get caught up in giving repetitive, nagging lectures that mean the child loses the plot!
- Speak in a calm, firm voice when you want something done.
- Try to get eye contact with your child when you are telling them to do something.
- Be consistent in what you will and won't allow.
  If one day you let your child take five chocolate biscuits, and the next day you say no chocolate biscuits, this can be a bit muddling in terms of boundaries.

- Try to explain or give reasons for decisions.
  Children can respond to fairness and logic and understand reasons if we give them.
- Be realistic in your expectations according to the age and stage of your child.
  It is no good expecting a two-year-old not to have a temper tantrum, but it would be reasonable for children to learn to control their tempers by seven or eight.
- Practise what you preach – set a good example.
  For example, if you don't want your kids to use abusive language, then don't use it yourself.
- Say sorry.
  If you have been unreasonable, moody or have shouted at the kids because of your own feelings, apologise – they can then learn to do this too!
- Remember children are their own people.
  Children have likes and dislikes and individual personalities and temperaments.
- Avoid using threats or shouting to control your child.
  Fear is not the best method of control.
- If a child behaves badly, avoid humiliating, rejecting or labelling them.
  Telling children that they are impossible, difficult or stupid can last a lifetime. Threatening to withdraw love can be extremely damaging to their security.
- When a child has done something wrong, tell them but also give them strategies as to what they could do differently in the future.
- Wait after arguments and tantrums until the child is calm enough for you both to discuss the problem.
- Be ready to sometimes renegotiate and compromise.
  Some things we can let go and they do not matter much in the long term – other behaviour we really need to be firm about.
- Try not to give a great deal of attention to poor behaviour.
  This gives the message to children that poor behaviour will gain them parent time. Don't ignore the behaviour, but be brief,

firm and calm. Explain to children what it is you need them to do and set clear boundaries.

- Remember that you are not alone.
  All parents struggle with their children's behaviour sometimes – it is part of being a parent and raising the human race!

7

Development of language skills – talking and listening

Talking and listening skills are essential for communication, relationships, social and learning development. Through talking, we can articulate our feelings, thoughts, interests, questions, learning, fears and dreams. We can convey important information and data about our world. Through listening, we can hear other people's feelings, thoughts, interests, questions, learning, fears and dreams. We can hear important information and data about their world. Being listened to and being heard are crucial to a child's development of self-worth and self-esteem. Through people listening to us, we learn that we have an opinion or thoughts worth listening to, and that we have feelings we can share.

School partnership

Schools realise the vital importance in the learning process of developing talking and listening skills and therefore they set up opportunities within the school day to allow children to be able to practise and refine their skills.

These skills will include the following:

Asking and answering questions

Children need to develop confidence to ask and answer questions within the classroom environment. The best environment allows children the opportunity to enquire and be curious and to seek answers to their questions. Children should feel able to take the risk and ask questions, even if they don't always get the answer right, and this means creating an environment of trust where it is OK to get it wrong.

Good teachers will make sure that all the children in the class have an opportunity to ask and answer questions on a regular basis as teaching is an interactive experience.

Talking about experiences

Part of talking is 'telling the story' of what has happened to you, and how you reacted or felt about it. Schools usually have a 'news time' when children are given the opportunity to talk about what is the news in their life and to share their feelings or reactions.

Learning to listen quietly while sitting in a group

Learning to listen and absorb information is a skill in itself. Children are by their nature active and find it difficult to sit still. However, if a classroom of thirty children is to remain calm and able to learn, then listening skills are a prerequisite. Children need to learn to sit still without fidgeting or shuffling. They need to look at the person speaking, or at the visual teaching material. They need to follow what is being said and absorb it, in such a way as to re-process it and answer questions the teacher may pose.

When children first enter school, teachers spend a great deal of time and energy focusing on listening skills and training children to sit cross-legged on a carpet, avoid touching one another, and maintain eye contact. In our culture, we have set ideas about what listening 'looks like'. As adults, after good early childhood training, even though minds may wander off into the middle distance, our bodies will remain in a listening pose that can deceive the speaker of our true attention levels. This focus on listening skills will lead into the literacy and numeracy hours, story time and all other times during the school day when the teacher wants to gain the attention of the children.

Children also have to learn to listen to the contributions of other children having their turn to talk and to show them respect by keeping quiet and attentive.

Development of vocabulary

Schools are language-rich environments where children are constantly learning new vocabulary, and expanding on their old one. They will learn the underlying concepts of grammatical structure and the names for words like nouns, verbs and adjectives. They will learn comparative language such as big, bigger, biggest, and will have an opportunity to use the mathematical language of measurement and number. Science has its own special vocabulary with practical experimentation.

Children also get an opportunity to explore books, listen to tapes, sing songs, learn rhymes and look at poetry. All of these enable their vocabulary and ability to express themselves to expand and mature.

Standing up and speaking

Children also have opportunities within school to stand up and talk about their learning, news or interests, and to therefore try out their talking skills on an audience. This can give children confidence that they have something worth saying and something worth explaining to others. As they get older, they may get an opportunity to speak out in a school assembly or in front of an assembled audience of parents and school community.

Learning when not to talk

Because of the number of children in a class, children have to learn when it is appropriate to talk and when it is not. They have to learn to take a turn, or wait for an opportunity to say something that they are burning to say! Often, the teacher will ask someone else to speak and a child will have to contain what it is he or she wants to talk about. This is an important lesson to learn; while we have a right and a need to talk, sometimes we must keep quiet or hold what we have to say until later or until another occasion.

Talking and learning

Nowadays, children are allowed for the most part to keep a low level of discussion with the pupils sitting directly around them. Classrooms are arranged in small sets of tables which are conducive to discussion and collaboration. The teacher will always encourage the discussion to be focused on the task in hand. This is because children can learn more through talking and discussing things among themselves than through remaining silent and getting on with the task on their own.

Home partnership

Encouraging your child to talk to you and listening to what they say are two essential building blocks for effective parenting. Remember that communication is the basis of all relationships and this is particularly so for the parent–child relationship. Often we find it difficult to listen to our children because we are so busy with the complex business of living, working, keeping the house clean, getting children to school etc. We let children's 'prattle' go in one ear and out the other. Sometimes it is just too difficult to listen. However, if we don't make time, some of the time, then our children will feel unheard, they will lack confidence and interest in others, and our relationship with them will deteriorate.

Asking and answering questions

An early word children learn is the question 'why?' Often, as parents, we get completely fed up of hearing the word 'why?', but asking questions shows curiosity, enquiry and an interest in the world around us. It is also a primary way in which children learn to talk and listen. In wanting to know the answer, they will want to listen to the answer.

When we ask children questions, we are then inviting them into conversation. We invite them to give an opinion, or their thoughts, and as such we give them status and self-worth: what they have to say is worth hearing.

Family listening time

Rather like 'news time' at school, it is good to set up talking and listening times in the home environment when there will be a space to talk and listen properly. Meal-time is the tradi-tional time when a family can sit down together and share their day with individual members of the family. You cannot do this with a television! As an adult, you can sometimes take the lead in sharing your news, reactions and feelings, therefore modelling this to your children. You can help children to show respect when other people are talking and to take their turn. This is an opportunity for listening as well as talking skills. Research has indicated that families who share a meal together each day are happier, healthier, more likely to have good relation-ships, and the children are less likely to exhibit behavioural difficulties. Could this have something to do with talking and listening?

Listening to the individual child

Another good slot in the day is when children are getting into bed, ready to settle down. It can be two minutes or ten minutes. This is a time for you to talk one-to-one with an individual child. The child can relax without competing for your time with siblings or the other responsibilities attached to adult life. It doesn't have to be serious or full of ponderous, worthwhile discussion, but it is a time when your child can feel you are available to them, and a time set apart especially for them to talk and you to listen. If a child knows you will set aside this 'special' time for them, then they can relax and hold on to things to talk about to you. It may help them not to be so attention seeking during the day.

Parents learning to stop, children learning to wait

Having said this, children do not always want to talk when we have allocated them a specific time. Their needs will interrupt our schedule and sometimes we will have to put our schedule aside to allow them to talk and for us to listen. If it is simply not possible to pay attention at that particular moment, it is good to give a reason why and to give your child a time when you will talk and listen and keep to your word. Children have to learn that there are sometimes better times to talk and be listened to than others.

How to encourage children to talk

Sometimes, we will want to talk and our children will clam up. A common parental experience being when we ask, 'What did you do at school today?' and our children give us the answer, 'Just stuff'! This can sometimes feel like rejection and we don't bother to ask again. Sometimes children just need time and a period of relaxation and closeness before they can chat to us. Often, sitting in the car going on a journey can encourage children to talk. Sometimes it is when we are engaged in other activities which still allow the opportunity for discussion. For example, when we are washing up and the child is sitting at the kitchen table drawing.

It is important, as parents, for us to understand what encourages children to communicate and how we can enhance that communication.

- When listening to your child, try to maintain eye contact wherever possible (not when you are driving!).
- Adopt a body-language posture that is similar to your child's. This is a way of demonstrating our empathy through mirroring body language.
- Respond by using a tone of voice lower than that of the child's – i.e. a quieter one in response to excited chatter. This will help reduce tension and/or temper in the child.
- Use body language to indicate that you are really listening – e.g., looking, nodding, leaning forward, using facial expressions to convey understanding.
- Give verbal feedback such as: 'yes, I see' or 'uhuh' or 'I understand' etc.
- Turn off the TV, stop what you are doing, and give your undivided attention.
- If you are not able to do so, arrange a later time when you will be less busy.
- Focus on what is being said, if you are not sure what is meant, reframe what has been said in your own words and ask the child if you have got it right.

Often children are more likely to talk if we use 'door openers' such as:

- Who?
- What?
- Why?
- How?
- Where?
- When?

We can then move the conversation forward with 'pathway questions' such as:

- How do you know?
- How did you find out?

- What do you think?
- What did it mean?
- How do you feel about it?

Using something called a 'reflective listening' approach can help children to sort out the 'story' they are telling and their feelings and thoughts about what they are talking about. This can involve either repeating or echoing back the last few words that a child has spoken, or giving a brief account of what has been said, outlining the main points or asking questions to clarify what you understand has been said. You can also suggest to the child how they might be feeling, e.g., 'it sounds like you are upset/angry/nervous'. This gives the child the opportunity to identify emotions and feelings and widens their emotional vocabulary.

Sometimes we can hinder our communication with children by not being prepared to hear what they are saying and by seeking our own agenda instead.

This can happen when:

- we give advice that hasn't been asked for – we're the grown-up, we must know best!
- we criticise the way the child behaved/reacted before they have had an opportunity to tell us why they behaved/reacted that way;
- we dismiss their feelings or emotions as being unimportant;
- we correct their grammar or the way they are speaking halfway through the conversation;
- we ignore them and carry on reading the newspaper, watching the telly, washing the floor;
- we reassure them that their fears can never happen when we know these things do happen in the real world;
- we praise them when they are quiet, withdrawn or passive for not bothering us.

Sometimes, our talking relationship with children can be limited to a series of commands which we issue rather like a sergeant major. The average parent gives up to seventeen commands in half an hour. Sometimes we will give one command after another: 'get out of bed', 'put your slippers on', 'don't forget your dressing gown', 'go and have a wash', 'remember to dry yourself properly', 'brush your teeth', 'brush your hair', etc. No wonder sometimes children can't remember what we have said and sometimes don't seem to be following instructions!

Language-rich home life

If we want our children to have a good vocabulary, conversational skills and the ability to discuss things, then we have to provide opportunities for this to happen within the home. These skills are not developed through watching television or playing computer games, but only in conversing with real human beings!

In the last few years, there has been an enormous growth in speech and language difficulties in young children. It is thought this is largely due to the majority of homes having the constant background noise of a television, radio, music or computer blaring out somewhere in the house. Babies and toddlers cannot screen out background noise fully until they are around three years old, so they are not able to hear, understand and pick up the language of speech from their environment in the way they could in the past. Instead of engaging with people, infants are often sat in front of the screen, watching TV or videos. These factors are having a disturbing long-term impact on children's future learning within school.

Children's vocabulary and ability to converse grows within the home through listening to adult conversation, talking to adults, engaging with adults, chatting to their friends, being read to, listening to tapes, playing games and reading for themselves. Some television programmes can be extremely informative, interesting and full of language learning but this probably doesn't include cartoons!

Having children who listen

If we can learn to listen to our children and model this behaviour they are far more likely to become good listeners themselves.

Children can learn to listen through listening to stories being read, quiet times of discussion, listening to tapes or stories on the radio, or listening to others talking. To listen we have to be able to be quiet, to concentrate, to shut out what else is happening in the room, and to focus on sound rather than vision or action. The more opportunities children have to do these things, the more they will be able to attend and listen in school.

There are other tips for getting children to listen:

- Say your child's name and get them to give you eye contact before you begin saying what it is you want them to listen to.
- Move closer to the child – shouting up the stairs or from room to room in the house often doesn't produce the best results!
- Use simple language or instructions rather than a whole, incomprehensible mouthful!
- Check for hearing and understanding – 'What have I just said/asked you to do?' This leaves much less room for the child to pretend they have not heard!
- Use body language as well as words to convey the message you want to give. If you are hesitant, or wavering on a behavioural issue, children will pick this up instantly and will 'listen' to your body language rather than your words.
- Make sure that your child is not just a listener in the family but has a chance to talk as well – sometimes one sibling can become the talker and the other, quieter, child the listener.

Both school and home have a huge role to play in encouraging the development of talking and listening skills. Parents can complement the role of schools by providing a home environment rich in conversation, talking, being listened to and being heard. Talking and listening skills are intrinsically connected to good social skills and the ability to learn and take in information.

8

Development of concentration and attention skills

The ability to concentrate and pay attention is vital to enable learning to take place. Many children who struggle in the school environment do so because they have poor attention and concentration skills. They are not able to focus on the task in hand without being easily distracted by what is going on around them, they are too aware of what other people are doing, or they spend their time restless and agitated or fidgeting. Apart from affecting their ability to absorb information and complete tasks, this lack of concentration and attention will probably cause behaviour that is unacceptable in the classroom and will get the child into trouble with the teacher. This can spiral downwards with children losing their self-esteem and motivation so the attention and concentration skills become even poorer.

When discussing concentration and attention skills, it is worthwhile to understand that we all have a preferred way of learning. This seems to be something we are born with and cannot change.

It does not mean we can't learn in other ways, it merely means that it is our preference to learn in a particular way.

These three ways of learning are:

Auditory learners – 30 per cent of the population

The auditory learner is most comfortable taking in information through listening to the spoken word. This type of learner is very at home in the classroom where many learning outcomes are dependent on listening ability.

Visual learners – 30 per cent of the population

The visual learner is more comfortable when information is displayed in a visual way through diagrams, flip charts, videos and illustrations. It is these that the visual learner notes, rather than the accompanying auditory information.

Kinaesthetic learners – 40 per cent of the population

The kinaesthetic (or movement) learner is an interactive practical learner. This type of learner learns best through practical activities with materials or interaction in drama or movement. Children who are kinaesthetic learners struggle most in the school environment. Sitting still, listening and concentrating in the manner expected in the classroom is a struggle. The kinaesthetic child would rather be up and doing, making and building, sorting or creating. These children are best doing practical activities where their attention and concentration skills are not in doubt and where they have the best chance of learning.

The good school environment will provide opportunities for all three learning preferences, making sure there is plenty of visual stimuli in the classroom as well as practical interactive tasks for children to do. However, it still remains that much of the National Curriculum is dependent on communicating information in an auditory way. Much of the literacy and numeracy hours in primary school are spent with children expected to sit quietly and attentively on a carpet and listen to the teacher giving out information and asking questions. This gives auditory learners a natural advantage. Visual learners, and particularly kinaesthetic learners, need to be taught skills of attention and concentration that do not come naturally to them. This skill-building can take place both in school and at home.

School partnership

From the moment children start school, teachers will focus on training them to sit still and listen attentively to their teaching, to stories or to discussions. They will give children a number of planned activities but encourage them to focus for increasing periods of time on a single activity. They will do this making their expectations clear through praise and encouragement, and maybe stickers or stars and positive feedback.

When they start school, many children like to flit from activity to activity, only staying in one place for a minute or two. They are naturally excited by the environment and want a little bit of everything. When reception classes were more an extension of nursery 'learning through play' environments, these children had an opportunity to slowly build up their ability to concentrate for longer on a given activity. Now, right from the beginning of schooling, children are expected to sit still for twenty to thirty minutes at a time. Many children, particularly kinaesthetic boys, find this almost impossible.

We must remember that top attention levels for extremely attentive adults is twenty minutes. Most of us will drift off into our own thoughts and concerns or be distracted by what is going on around us or by what other people are doing. Therefore children whose level of concentration is naturally much lower will need constant encouragement to stop them drifting away and enable them to focus back on the task in hand.

Good teaching staff will give feedback every few minutes such as: 'well done for listening', 'I can see you are working really hard', etc., which draws the child back on task. Staff can prolong children's interest in an activity by encouraging them to expand on what they are doing 'just a little bit more' or to 'just try a bit longer'.

Good schools will recognise that their kinaesthetic learners can concentrate and attend when building models, cooking, playing the drums, painting or playing sport. They will raise children's self-esteem and ability in these activities, keeping their motivation higher when things are more difficult for them, for example concentrating on a mathematical activity.

One of the essentials of children being able to concentrate and complete tasks is being able to understand that a task has a beginning, a middle and an end, and being able to assess how long each of these processes will take. Often, children have difficulty in setting down to a task and need help and support to do this. Sometimes, children get 'stuck' in the middle of a task and need moving on. At others, children cannot put on that extra spurt to complete a task successfully (these are the children who find themselves staying in at lunchtime to finish their work). The job of the good teacher is to understand the needs of different children so they can be offered the appropriate support at the right time. Some teachers will give children times when they expect, for example, one or two sentences to have been completed. Others will stop the children and ask where they have got to and remind them how long they have got in which to complete the task. Again, praise and encouragement provide the motivation to refocus the non-attentive learner.

Another key ingredient in the ability to concentrate is being able to block out what is going on around you and to focus on what it is you have to do. This can be very difficult in a classroom where there are maybe thirty to thirty-five people also engaged in a number of tasks. Some may be chattering, the teacher may be explaining things to a small group, some may be wandering about, and someone else is sharpening their pencil, etc. Children need practice and positive feedback to shut out distractions and to keep focused. The sympathetic teacher will realise that some children will only develop these skills by being given a space to work that is away from distractions. Rather than being punitive, a work station on its own in a quiet corner can be a way for children to build up attention and focusing skills.

Home partnership

Children will be at very different levels of concentration and attention skills when they enter school. Children who have had an early opportunity to build up these skills in nursery or in the home environment will be at a natural advantage. Parents can complement the school's role in building concentration and attention in a multitude of ways.

We can identify the natural preference of the way our children learn – although many children seem to be kinaesthetic because they are constantly on the move, we also notice if our children particularly enjoy visual stimuli or listening to music and tapes.

We can provide activities for our children that demand attention to complete – such as jigsaws or building materials like Lego or Knex. We can sit beside them and encourage them to start, pursue and finish activities. When they are immersed in something and refuse to be distracted from it, we can praise them for their attention and ability to focus. When they want to leave something half done, we can encourage them to go the extra mile to finish it. Doing two activities at once, for example you reading a story while they listen and draw a picture, can help children focus on two tasks simultaneously.

Reading stories, playing games and interacting with your children all build attention and concentration. If your child is able to sit playing on the floor with toys, telling a story, imagining scenarios while the business of the world is going on around them, then they are showing signs that they can block out distractions and focus. Kinaesthetic children may not want to do this sitting around being imaginative stuff and be constantly on the move instead! Try structured activities such as dance, cooking, swimming club, martial arts, trampolining or football – all of which require concentration and learning systematic routines (with a beginning, middle and end) while being active.

9

Development of reading skills

Learning to read is one of the most important foundation blocks for success in life. So much information, learning and enjoyment comes to us through the written word that without literacy we would be fairly lost in the modern world. Most parents have high expectations that their children will go to primary school and, if nothing else, learn to read. Reading is the gateway to information, but also to a great deal of pleasure and relaxation. Through being able to read, we can enter other worlds and other people's minds, thoughts and feelings. We can be excited, enchanted, amazed, gripped and absorbed by a good story. If you enjoy reading a book, you can never be bored in life because there will always be another good book to get into.

Reading is also the foundation for much of our children's learning in school. Children will have to read off the board, read text books, read questions, read information on the Internet, read their own writing, etc. They need to understand the meaning of what they read and why they like or don't like it. They need to explore a variety of reading materials such as stories, poems, dictionaries and encyclopaedias.

So how do children learn to read? There are still many respected academics who argue out exactly how children acquire the skills of reading. There are two main methodologies that historically have fought it out in educational circles. The first is a belief that children learn by 'look and say', that is, children look at a word, learn to recognise its shape and associate it with the picture of the word in their head. For example, when they see the word elephant, next to a picture of an elephant, they learn to associate the shape of this word with an elephant. The second is a belief that children learn by building up words through 'phonics'. That is, as they learn the sound of each individual alphabet letter and then the sound combinations that a number of letters make together, they are able to build up words and sound them out. The truth of the matter is that children are individuals who learn in different ways and probably use a combination of the two. We need to provide them with opportunities to do both.

The essential requisite for learning to read is practice, practice and more practice. If there is a secret to learning to read, it is quite simply to do it. The more children do it, the better they will get along. Unfortunately, there are many distractions for today's children in starting to read for themselves and enjoying the process. We are now a world full of visual stimuli such as television or computer games which often prove more attractive to children who find reading more of a challenge. This means they read less and therefore fall further behind in competency.

Sadly, it is still a reality that many children leave primary school with poor reading skills and this has a profound impact on their secondary education. It is difficult then to catch up as so much of the curriculum is dependent on being able to read, so young people fall more and more behind their peer group. Children who leave school with poor reading skills are much less likely to gain good employment and more likely to show criminal behaviour. Our prisons are full of men and women who are semi-literate. Many of them will have dyslexia or some other learning difficulty that was not sufficiently addressed when they were little.

School partnership

Once we can read, it seems like a simple task, but in fact it is an incredibly complex skill, made up of many different skills, that together allow us to interpret letters into words, words into sentences and sentences into text. From the moment children enter school, they are immersed in a process of acquiring this range of skills. As children travel from the infant department and through the juniors, these skills will include:

Infants

- how to handle and care for books;
- an understanding that a book works from front to back;
- an understanding that print goes from left to right;
- an understanding that the pictures hold clues about the story;
- learning to associate print with the picture;
- learning to associate what is being said with the print;
- opportunities to talk and reflect on a story;
- opportunities to see patterns or repetitions in a story-line;
- shape recognition of letters and words;
- simple beginning sounds of their own name;
- recognition of their own first name in writing;
- recognising letters and initial sounds;
- recognising and putting together different sounds such as 'sh', 'ch' and 'br' (phonics);
- learning endings to words like 'ing'.
- being able to sound out words;
- reading simple beginner books;
- recognising some words;
- reading sentences;
- developing an ever-increasing reading vocabulary;
- reading nursery and modern rhymes;
- looking at simple non-fiction books;
- reading simple story books with illustrations.

Junior skills

- reading longer books with fewer illustrations;
- studying stories and language from different cultures;
- learning to use an index, glossary, dictionary and contents page;
- reading poetry, stories and information texts;
- making sense of instructions and explanations in books;
- reading with increasing fluency and competence;
- understanding that there are different kinds of reading materials – fiction, non-fiction, reference, plays, poetry, etc.;
- the ability to use a good dictionary and thesaurus;
- the ability to look up things in directories and encyclopaedias;
- being able to show some early critical appreciation of different authors and poets;
- reading books without illustrations;
- answering comprehension questions on what he or she has read.

Schools help children to acquire these skills through a number of different ways. Good schools are 'reading rich' environments full of good quality, well-illustrated children's books. On display boards and walls there should be evidence of the promotion of reading skills.

In every primary school, the National Curriculum demands that children take part in a 'literacy hour' in the morning – this consists of roughly four slots covering the following areas:

1. Whole-class shared reading or writing. This will mean a structured session with the teacher, possibly practising phonics (sounding out the letter combinations that construct words) or reading a large text book together.
2. Whole-class word and sentence work – this could mean looking at grammar and punctuation.
3. Group and individual reading and writing tasks.
4. Whole-class talking about what has been done and learned.

Most infant classrooms will have a book or reading 'corner' with cushions or small seats to allow children to sit comfortably while they look at books or read them. In the early years, a wide variety of picture books arranged in an accessible way will attract children.

Books with visual impact and good, bright illustrations will tempt the non-reader to want to acquire the skill of reading.

Early year classrooms will also have a 'carpet' or 'mat' area where the children gather as a group to listen to a member of staff tell a story sometime during the day. Listening to stories and looking at illustrations is a shared pleasure for the whole class. Everyone loves a story. As children get older, the teacher may read a chapter from a longer book each day.

There are many fun-and-games-type activities in the early years that children enjoy, but also improve their reading skills. These might include letter and picture lotto games or sequencing games – such as 'I went to market and I bought . . .' Creative activities are also included, for example, children enjoy making their own simple books out of paper and card.

As children get older, there will be class reading of classic fiction, poetry or drama. Pupils will explore myths, legends, parables and fables. They will also be encouraged to explore a range of different types of reading materials such as advertisements, circulars and newspaper and magazine articles.

Most schools will establish a time of 'quiet reading' every day, often after lunch, when children are encouraged to sit down and get on with actually reading a book of their own choice, on their own. During this time, teachers, assistants and parent helpers may hear individuals read out loud to them. It is recognised that the more children have an opportunity to practise reading, the more likely they are to become fluent, confident readers.

Home partnership

Reading is an area where, as parents, we can make a huge difference to our children's skill development. Our attitude to books and to reading will profoundly influence our children's attitude to learning to read and to getting long-term pleasure from reading.

We need to decide whether or not our homes are 'reading rich' environments where children can pick up the importance and joy of the written word. First of all, when children watch us read and enjoy a good book, or settle down to read the Sunday newspapers, they are getting messages that reading is an interesting and enjoyable pursuit.

We all have access to local libraries that, on the whole, have an up-to-date range of good children's books. When we take our children to the library to choose a book and we choose a book for ourselves as well, we are again modelling reader-type behaviour. It is possible to buy cheap books for children at jumble sales, car boot sales and charity shops, often in very good condition, which can give a great deal of pleasure. Books and book tokens make great presents to ask for at Christmas or birthdays and will probably last a lot longer than some toy that falls out of favour.

If you look at the lists of skill development, you will see that there are many areas where you can help at home. Among them are respect for books, enjoyment of books and reading, and training children to link print with story and information. We can sing nursery rhymes and teach simple songs to children. Research has also shown that children who can repeat rhymes acquire reading skills more quickly.

Reading stories to children at bedtime (or at other times) can be a deeply enjoyable process for both of you. It brings you closer, and allows you to share a story and/or pictures together. Many children's books have sophisticated messages 'between the lines' which, like all good literature, allow them to be understood at different levels of maturity of understanding.

When children are ready to start reading, they will let you know by asking what certain words are, or how to sound words out. You can then support and encourage them. You can help them sound letters phonically and point out when a word rhymes or has the same ending as another one. Most children brought up in 'reading rich' environments will be eager to learn to read and decipher the words which will mean they can 'hear' the story for themselves whenever they want.

Bringing reading books home will probably be the first 'homework' your child is given at school. Beware of reading becoming a battle or chore for both of you, otherwise children will set up resistance to the activity and be less and less likely to do it. As always, encouragement and praise when they are successful is the best way forward. Sometimes, the offer of reading a book to them if they will read a book to you first, can work.

It is useful to set up a structured time to do reading together. This signals to your child that this is an important activity you wish to support them in. The right time for your child might vary. Sometimes it is after your child has had time to eat and play a little – or it could be before bedtime or in the morning before they go to school. Some children enjoy doing 'paired' reading – you read a little bit, then they read a little bit. Some children will benefit from you saying a word when they are stuck; occasionally, it is better to challenge them to try to sound it out. Little and often is the key to reading practice. Two or three minutes twice a day can be better than one slot of twenty minutes when the child gets cross and fed up with doing it and you both fall out.

If your child does not seem to be progressing very well in reading, despite enjoying hearing stories read and looking at pictures, if they also seem to be struggling at writing and spelling, you may need to investigate whether they have some kind of specific learning difficulty that might be getting in the way.

10

Development of writing skills

Writing is the other side of literacy development and, again, it is an incredibly important basic skill for our children to acquire. Writing is a primary medium by which we communicate information and learning, problem solve and give our reflections, thoughts and feelings. Through writing, we can tell our own 'story'. Writing is made up of a whole range of complex individual skills that together allow us to put pen to paper. There is the skill of actually forming letters in the correct way and joining them up to make words, there is the skill of spelling those words in the right way, and then there is the whole business of developing writing fluency and competency to express ourselves through the written word.

In our present education system, with its test/exam-based written assessment, the reality is that writing is all-important to success. Children are expected to write down what they know. Even if they could answer every question given verbally with incredible accuracy, clarity and good articulation, this would not be enough. Tests, such as SATs and the exams of the future, must be read and then answered in writing. Our society assesses children not on what they know but what they are able to write down. This puts children with writing or spelling difficulties in a unfortunate position. Although there is more understanding about dyslexic problems than ever before, this is not really taken into consideration when it comes to testing what they know.

So how do we learn to write? As we know, all young children enjoy drawing and painting – making their mark on paper (or sometimes on the wall) and writing is an extension of drawing in the sense that letters are markings with meanings. Children gradually acquire an understanding of the meaning of these markings as they develop reading skills in conjunction with writing skills. Children cannot write until they have developed sufficient hand control to hold a pencil and can determine how it moves about on the page. Writing too is a matter of practice, practice and more practice. The more adept children become at forming letters, the easier it will be to join them together to make words and then sentences. Writing fluency only comes when children no longer have to concentrate on how letters and words are formed – their hand automatically forms them – and their writing flow can keep in line with their thoughts.

School partnership

Schools set out to teach children a whole range of skills that will enable them to work towards writing fluency and competency. The purpose of writing is communication, but our written communication is very different from communication through the spoken word, and children need to acquire the complexity of new rules and structures.

These are some of the skills needed to write that are taught within the primary school:

Infants

- holding the pencil the right way;
- hand control – writing requires hand co-ordination and flexibility;

- developing drawing skills;
- being able to colour in without going over the lines;
- forming letters the right way;
- forming words;
- spelling simple words;
- writing sentences with spaces between words;
- learning basic spelling rules;
- learning basic punctuation, such as capital letters and full stops;
- writing stories by hand and on computer.

Schools will supply children with a wide range of drawing and writing implements to give them opportunities to make their 'mark' on paper. They might experiment with wax crayons, charcoal, coloured pencils, felt pens and biros, all of which make different kinds of marking. Painting with a selection of different coloured paints and different-size brushes again gives children the chance to explore making an impression on paper.

If your child takes a pencil case to school, make sure that the contents are in good condition. Pencils will need regular sharpening to remain useful and felt-pens will be dried out if all the tops are left off. It is better to buy cheap and cheerful versions as children inevitably lose them.

Hand control can be developed through activities that require the hands to use small, complex manipulation and movement. Activities such as bead-threading or making patterns with small pegs in pegboards. Young children will practise colouring basic shapes or tracing over simple drawings. This increases children's control over the pencil they are holding.

Teachers will focus on how letters are formed in the literacy hour and children will learn to copy their formations, drawing in sand, paint and on paper. When young children begin to want to write simple sentences, they might dictate something to the teacher and then write over the letters that the teacher has written. This will be followed by writing underneath adult script before they begin to write independently.

Quite early on, children begin to realise that a word must be spelt in a certain way to be 'right'. Unfortunately, in the English language, phonically sounding out words does not always work as there are so many exceptions to rules.

Schools will encourage children to take pride in their writing and to see it as a way of communication that can be read by other people. Good schools will display children's writing in classrooms and public areas such as corridors and halls.

Different schools have different ideas as to how children should be taught handwriting. Some like children to start joining up letters right from the beginning to encourage early fluency in writing style. Others feel that children must be competent at forming individual letters before they move on to joined-up writing. Certainly, many children see joined-up writing as a rite of passage.

Similarly, most children will write in pencil to begin with, which is easy to rub out and does not require the same kind of hand control and paper pressure as a pen. When they begin to write more fluently children move on to writing in ink. It is a big moment when we go out to buy their first pen.

These are some of the skills which older children learn within the primary school:

Juniors

- increasing vocabulary, using more interesting, complex and a greater variety of words;
- choosing words and details to interest the reader;
- good sentence construction;
- knowledge of spelling and spelling rules;
- all basic punctuation rules;
- handwriting with fluency and legibility;
- joined-up writing;
- writing with pen rather than pencil;
- writing stories with a beginning, middle and an end;
- composing poems;
- writing answers to questions;

- writing for different purposes, such as lists or instructions;
- being able to write in paragraphs;
- developing different writing styles – poetry, fiction and non-fiction;
- answering comprehension questions.

Juniors will engage in a whole range of writing activities throughout the school day, not just in the literacy hour. They will be expected to learn spellings and to do spelling tests. They will practise handwriting – many schools have a formulaic writing style that they encourage children to follow. During literacy hour, teachers will focus on doing whole-class activity, for example, looking at a particular grammatical, spelling or punctuation rule. Children will then do follow-up activities to expand their writing competency.

Parent partnership

As with reading, parents can do a great deal to support their children's writing development and ability. They can offer paper and different drawing mediums to children, and can beg, borrow and scrounge paper from various different sources. Many companies throw out bags of scrap paper every day. Children don't mind if there is meaningless print on one side of the paper.

We can help develop their hand control by encouraging them to do activities that will enhance their ability to manipulate small objects. This could be activities such as making coloured paper mosaics, cutting out and sticking, or, once again, building with Duplo, Lego or Knex. Colouring in, although sometimes seeming a bit meaningless, is a way in which children learn to keep within the lines. Joining up the dots on a dot-to-dot, as well as improving number skills, is a pencil-control exercise. This is a development of hand control. There are many early writing exercise books to be found in bookshops which children don't perceive as work but as challenging fun.

As they get older, children can be encouraged to write as much as possible through being asked to write down lists or phone messages. Some children will enjoy writing letters to friends or grandparents who live far away. Especially if they receive letters back – everyone likes the excitement of getting a letter. An old-fashioned concept, but writing thank-you letters delights the giver of presents and will usually ensure another one in the future!

One way of extending children's writing ability is to allow them to dictate to you while you type or write their story and then allow them to copy it. This divorces the skill of handwriting and spelling from the skills of the creative process. Often, children find the process of writing so slow and cumbersome it cannot keep up with the flow of the ideas in their head and this can be frustrating if they have lots of ideas to communicate. You can then ask them who actually 'wrote' the story, even though you took the dictation. They will then begin to realise the most important part of being able to write things down is to communicate what we want to say. Handwriting and spelling skills will mature and come gradually, but we must be careful not to put children off the communication of their ideas, thoughts and what they know.

Learning spellings is something that parents can help and support with. Helping children to sound out words phonically so they can remember the composite parts of a word is helpful, as is their looking at the shape of the word and associating it in their mind with an object if it is a noun. Putting up the words individually on a pin board in their bedroom can help them to go over them during the course of a week. Remembering spellings is very much a 'visualisation' technique. It is like putting the spelling on a white board or screen in your brain so that you can recall it and match it, letter to letter, when you write it down again. Some children find it very difficult to spell out loud, ordering letters in their mind, but find it easier to write the word down when they can tell whether it is 'right' or not. There are some good computer spelling programmes on the market that can help children as they can do them quietly and without the pressure of adult intervention.

Spelling usually improves as children become more adept at reading and therefore have more experience of seeing words spelt correctly on a regular basis. Therefore the more we manage to get our children to read, the better their spelling is likely to be.

If your child seems to find spelling extremely difficult and can't remember how things are spelt from one week to the next, then you may need to explore the possibility of their having a learning difficulty.

11

Development of number skills

We all use number skills through the course of every day. It is impossible not to, whether it's estimating the time it will take to get to places, working out money change, or laying the table for the right number of people. In an increasingly technological age it is the backbone of many of the ways we operate in today's society. Everywhere we look we see numbers in action. We can notice shape, the organisation of space and measurement all around us. Mathematics provides logic, structure and order to the universe and underpins all scientific theory. In order to build and make things, we have to be able to estimate and measure up materials. We also have to be able to order them in the right quantities, and so on.

Although we now have many helpful additions to the mathematical process such as calculators and computers, children still need to understand underlying mathematical concepts in order to use them effectively. This means using mathematical concepts in the everyday practical world as well as transferring them into symbols, diagrams, words and numbers on paper.

School partnership

Primary schools set out to give children the basic mathematical conceptual skills which will underpin the more complex problem-solving and abstract theory that will follow at the secondary stage of education. There will be a gradual building up of these skills through the years of primary education. Each year children make huge strides forward in their mathematical understanding and these are like building blocks leading on to the next stage. If a child has not fully understood one stage, then it will be difficult for them to proceed to the next stage.

Schools need to be 'maths rich' environments with number friezes on the wall, times tables posters and displays of children's shape constructions or graph work. Here are some examples of some of the learning that will be taking place within the numeracy hour and beyond. This is by no means a comprehensive list, but it will give you a flavour of the breadth of the curriculum:

Infants

Reception class

- how to sort and match like things together, e.g. red things and blue things;
- knowing the names of numbers;
- how to count up to ten (or even twenty!);
- how to touch objects and count up to five;
- how to order things into tall, taller, tallest;
- the meaning of comparison words such as big and small, heavy and light, thick and thin. An understanding that three people will need three ice-creams;
- ability to see basic patterns, e.g. yellow, orange, yellow, orange, etc.;
- recognition of shapes, e.g. circle, square and triangle;
- recognition of a range of coins – 1p, 2p, 5p, 10p;
- some early time concepts;
- beginning to add and subtract.

Year 1
- counting up to twenty, and down again;
- putting numbers in the right order;
- adding and subtracting numbers under twenty;
- beginning to be able to add and subtract in their head (mental arithmetic);
- knowing which numbers add up to ten;
- telling the time when the clock strikes the hour or half hour.

Year 2
- being able to count to a hundred;
- beginning to do simple multiplication sums;
- understanding what double and half mean;
- knowing the two, five and ten times table by heart;
- being able to use a ruler to measure things;
- being able to explain to someone else how to do a maths problem.

In the infants, mathematical learning will be connected as much as possible with interactive practical activities. Children learn as they play, experiment and problem-solve with different materials.

This will include activities such as sorting things by colour or shape; making patterns with different coloured beads; playing dice games; investigating geometric and solid shapes; playing with pegboards and pegs, or plastic coins; learning the time on plastic clocks; and using weighing scales and metre rulers.

When you visit an infant classroom or playground, you might observe activities set up to encourage children to absorb mathematical concepts. These might include a colour display table, a pretend shop corner, number and counting rhymes being said or sung, or an outside play area with number ladders or hopscotch marked out. During the numeracy hour, children will be involved in tasks such as practising writing numbers in both number and spelt-out word form. Children could be making solid shapes from card or symmetrical shapes and patterns, they could be weighing and measuring, or learning and practising multiplication tables.

They might be using coloured cubes or rods to help them add and subtract. The numeracy hour will almost certainly involve whole-class counting or mental arithmetic. Children will be doing activities like making simple graphs, that demonstrate their favourite colours, for example. This will lead onto more abstract symbolic representations of mathematical thinking.

Here are some examples of learning taking place within the numeracy hour among older primary school children:

Juniors

Years 3 & 4
- reading and writing whole numbers up to a thousand;
- knowing the two, three, four, five and ten times table by heart;
- understanding pounds and pence and how to use them;
- understanding division and recognising simple fractions like ⅓ and ¹⁄₁₀;
- finding lines of symmetry using numbers in lists, tables and graphs;
- choosing and using the right method of solving a maths problem;
- using symbols like = correctly;
- adding and subtracting numbers in double figures without pen and paper;
- telling the time.

Years 5 & 6
- multiplying and dividing numbers up to a thousand;
- knowing all their tables;
- understanding decimals like 0.1 and 0.01;
- rounding up and down to the nearest ten, hundred or thousand;
- doing long multiplication (but not long division);
- recognising parallel lines;
- being competent at the 24-hour clock;
- understanding percentages as the number of units in every hundred;

- finding co-ordinates on graphs;
- solving problems by getting information from tables, graphs and charts.

In the Juniors, children will still be involved in active practical mathematical activities, but will also be expected to become more competent in mental arithmetic and applying mathematical concepts to abstract problem-solving. They will be following a mathematics text book and learning to lay out their work in a maths book. There is a great deal of whole-class work in the numeracy hour as this has been shown to be the most effective way of teaching mathematical concepts, but children may well be streamed across their age group as mathematical ability varies so dramatically within one group of children that it is difficult to meet their needs without dividing the most able from those who struggle with the subject area.

Home partnership

There are many everyday ways in which we can support the development of mathematical thinking. For example, laying the table (working out how many forks, knives, glasses, etc. are needed for each person), counting loose change, shopping, singing counting songs, and timing how long it takes for a child to complete a task. We can also get children to measure and weigh things – cooking can be a very good opportunity to practise maths in an enjoyable way.

When it comes to learning tables, there are good musical tapes on the market that you and your child can sing along to. Practising tables when you are going along in the car can be fun. Take it in turns to say the next line.

We can also get our children to notice shapes in the environment around them – how many squares, circles and triangles can they notice on the way to the shops or going along in the car?

Helping sort different types of groceries into different cupboards or the fridge is a sorting activity that defines objects into different areas. If children have to 'share' some sweets with siblings, then they will have to work out how everyone gets an equal amount (or there will be trouble!). Whenever an opportunity arises for children to be involved in the everyday maths of home, then you as a parent can utilise these opportunities to improve their mathematical thinking.

Games can also be a good way of learning numbers. Snakes and Ladders involves counting up and down. All double-dice games involve counting. There is a good counting game for very young children called 'Ladybirds', which involves counting dice and ladybirds in order to win.

Telling the time is another essential mathematical concept. Buy a big clock for the kitchen or their bedroom and get them to tell you the time starting with 'on the hour'. You can then ask questions such as: 'How long have we got before we have to leave for school if we are leaving at 8.30?' when they are a little older.

Fractions can be demonstrated in a practical way when we have to divide a cake or tart into the necessary portions to serve the number of people present. You can then ask children what fraction of the cake have they got if there are eight pieces.

Many children really enjoy the challenge of mathematics and they will see even more sense to it if you weave it into their everyday experiences.

12

Development of scientific understanding

Science is the study of how the world works. It is the subject that asks the big questions and tries to give answers. Scientific curiosity and understanding is vital in the modern world. We live in an age and society of fast-track scientific development. Every year there are new discoveries in the fields of physics, chemistry, biology and engineering that impact the way we live, from advances in technology to reproduction. Science graduates are highly valued in the job market. In primary school, children learn the basics of scientific enquiry. They discover how to answer questions by finding things out, experimentation and looking at the evidence. They learn how to devise tests and experiments to test out their theories and prove something, and they learn how to evaluate and write down their scientific methodology.

School partnership

Good schools encourage curiosity and a desire to know the answer to questions. They allow children to be imaginative in testing materials and their properties and in understanding physical processes such as forces, lights and sounds. They allow children to interact with their environment to promote scientific knowledge and understanding.

The curriculum will include the following, although this is not a comprehensive list:

Infants

- how to sort, group and describe objects and materials;
- how to do a simple scientific experiment and then be able to record and interpret the result in pictorial form or in a few sentences;
- understanding how animals and humans grow and develop, and what they eat;
- understanding how plants grow and reproduce;
- understanding how different species support life in a single habitat;
- how to care for the environment;
- how and why things die and decay;
- being able to observe and record different kinds of weather;
- being able to collect and examine objects and life from the natural world – e.g. leaves, wood, soil, rocks, plants and insects;
- an understanding of forces which pull, push and stop objects;
- a basic understanding of electricity, light and sound;
- an understanding of the marine and river world and the importance of water to sustain life;
- an understanding of the idea that objects can change their shape and form when cooled or heated, e.g. ice, water, wax and chocolate;
- a knowledge and understanding of various sources of light, of shadows, reflection and colour;
- a knowledge and understanding of scientific language.

Looking around a typical infant classroom, you might observe some of the following:

- children involved in topic work, exploring a subject area such as the weather or food;
- posters, artwork and graphs supporting the topic;
- a nature or science table focusing on the project;
- plants growing in the classroom from seed;
- a tank with frog spawn growing in the classroom;
- models children have made to illustrate forces or electricity;
- children doing simple experiments in pairs or groups;
- children making things with buzzers, bulbs, batteries and wires;
- cooking in groups;
- children studying things collected from trips to nearby habitats, e.g. the park or local woodland;
- paint-mixing activities to make colour combinations;
- children measuring with palms or feet or weighing scales;
- children measuring liquids in different containers to test their capacity.

Juniors

As children get older, more will be expected of them in terms of the thoroughness of their scientific methodology and collection of evidence. Schools aim to enable them to:

- be able to take a systematic and detailed approach to scientific investigation;
- be able to hypothesise when approaching an experiment as to its probable result;
- be able to record the experiment through diagrams, graphs and writing;
- use books and computers to explore further knowledge on a topic.

Examples of what might be observed in the junior classroom:

- children involved in a topic, e.g. farming or a woodland habitat;
- children doing chemical experiments to explore changes in everyday materials, e.g. firing clay;

- children investigating the properties of everyday materials such as weight,
- volume, strength and solubility;
- children exploring the properties of magnetic and non-magnetic materials;
- children exploring how light passes through lenses, prisms and filters.

Home partnership

The average home and garden provide a huge range of opportunities for children to carry out scientific research without you even realising it.

Playing in the bath with a range of different toys gives the opportunity to explore what sinks and floats. You can discuss what is it that seems to make an object float. If you give children a range of different-size plastic bottles, they can see how different-size containers can hold different amounts of liquid.

Cooking provides an opportunity for chemistry in action. What happens when we make a cake? The flour, eggs, butter and sugar are changed into something else through the process of mixing and heat. How come water can be three different things – steam when we boil a kettle, water in the tap and ice in the freezer? What happens when we leave food out, or in the fridge, for too long?

The garden provides children with an opportunity to plant seeds and watch them grow. Growing cress on cotton wool on the kitchen window sill and then making an egg-and-cress sandwich can be a chance to learn about growing food to eat. How about getting a tomato bag and watching tomatoes grow?

Keeping pets can allow children to understand how animals grow and develop and need particular food and habitat to be healthy. It can also be a way of coming to terms with the concept of death. Television has many wonderful nature programmes that give us an opportunity to observe animals operating in their natural habitat and raising their young.

When we talk to our children about puberty, sex and relationships, we are also giving them a science lesson in biological reproduction and what it involves!

There are also many places to visit which can give our children insight into scientific discovery and knowledge. The Science Museum in London has wonderful interactive displays for children, but there are also countless nature reserves, water and flour mills, farms and maritime museums which all give an opportunity for children to learn more about the world around them.

13

Development of historical understanding

We can only get a comprehensive sense of the present if we have an understanding and knowledge of the past. How did we get here? Who came before us? When were things built or discovered? History informs children about the world of the past so they can take part in the present and the future with a wisdom and knowledge of humankind. Piecing together the past is a bit like doing a jigsaw puzzle; each little bit that we know allows us to see more of the whole picture.

Children need to discover for themselves where our knowledge of the past comes from and learn how to weigh up the evidence to make theoretical assumptions about the way people lived their lives.

Schools allow children to develop their historical perspective through topic work that will capture their imagination about the past. A whole range of resources is used such as picture books, artefacts from the past, looking things up on the Internet, history wall-friezes that put events into chronological order and storytelling. Good schools will also arrange visits to museums and historical sites so children can have an opportunity to see reality-type glimpses of the past.

School partnership

Some of the skills being developed will include:

Infants

- an awareness of the past and an understanding of how it differs from the present and the future;
- use of words about the passing of time such as before, after, a long time ago, or in the past when . . .
- an understanding that things were different in the past, e.g. different clothes, different transport, or different kinds of entertainment;
- an understanding of the notion of a 'family tree';
- knowledge about some famous historical figures;
- the realisation that people acted in the way they did because of the times in which they lived;
- a sense of 'a very long time ago' (dinosaurs) and the close past (when Mummy was little).

If you visited an infant classroom, you might observe:

- children doing topics about things such as 'my school' with old photographs, or 'toys and games' that children used to play with;
- children doing a simple two-generational family tree;
- children celebrating events such as bonfire night and learning about a man called Guy Fawkes.

Juniors

Juniors will be concentrating on developing their notions of the past by studying particular periods of history and getting a sense of how people lived during these times.

Skills being developed will include:

- the ability to focus on famous people of the past and have an understanding of the time they lived and why they behaved as they did;
- an understanding of different historical periods in British history;
- an understanding of the foundations of our own culture through a knowledge and understanding of ancient history;
- an understanding of how people find out about the past from buildings, archaeology and ancient writings;
- the ability to find things out from encyclopaedias, the Internet and reference books about the past.

What you might see in a typical junior classroom:

- children studying and investigating topics about Roman Britain, Ancient Greece, Anglo-Saxons, Ancient Egypt, Vikings, Tudor and Stuart Times, Victorian Britain, World War Two;
- children dressing up for a 'Victorian Day' in school where they behave as if they were in Victorian times for the day;
- posters, photographs and artefacts that illustrate a particular period in history;
- children's artwork that illustrates their topic.

Home partnership

There are many ways in which we can support the development of our children's concept of the past. The first is by recognising that families themselves have a huge amount of history. A sense of the past can come very early when children look through photograph albums of themselves as babies and toddlers and realise they are different now to how they were then. In our fast-changing world, things such as clothes, hairstyles, furniture, shops and houses were all different when we were children, and grandparents also have much to offer in explaining to children what things were like when they were young. Often, families will have treasure troves of old photographs, medals and other artefacts that can give children insights into the past. Children are fascinated by how clothes and houses looked different, and by the way things were in 'old-fashioned' homes and schools.

We can help our children notice things in the world around them and be able to judge whether buildings are old or new. We can take them to old buildings such as churches or extraordinary sites such as Stonehenge. Many towns and cities have their own museums which give a historical perspective on local history.

Children will often bring topic work home, and this is an opportunity for parents to share investigation work into the past. We can help children look up information in encyclopaedias, go to the local library and get illustrated books on a period, or use the Internet to find pictures and text about a particular historical figure or event.

14

Development of geographical knowledge and understanding the world

Geographical knowledge and understanding of the world covers a wide range of skills, from where places are in the UK, Europe and other continents, to the way landscapes are formed and the effects of weather and climate. The world is becoming a smaller and smaller place. Cheap air transport and greater prosperity has meant that travel to distant places has become more common-place than ever before. Worldwide communications mean that we know what is going on around the world almost straightaway. Children need to have some knowledge of the wider world as well as an understanding of the environment on their front doorstep.

School partnership

Schools develop geographical understanding through the use of topic work and practical interaction with the local environment in which the community exists. Good schools will have posters, illustrations and reference books that reflect the wider global family and different environments.

Geographical skills will be slowly developed from infants to juniors in the following ways:

Infants

- by learning how to use simple maps – maybe from home to school;
- measuring and recording weather observations – sunny, windy, cloudy, etc.;
- gaining an understanding of the small locality in which they live;
- being able to name and understand geographical forms such as hills, mountains, streams, rivers, lakes, seas and oceans, through looking at pictures;
- gaining an understanding of how plants and trees are different from each other in different parts of the countryside and the world;
- gaining an understanding of how soil and rocks look and feel different;
- gaining an understanding of the difference between villages, towns and cities and the countryside;
- gaining an understanding of different forms of transport;
- learning how to recognise places on a map, e.g. England, Scotland, Wales and Ireland, and knowing which one they live in;
- gaining an understanding of how people affect the environment in which they live.

In the infant environment you would expect to find children involved in the following activities:

- projects or topic work based on subjects such as the seasons, things that grow, where I live, how I get to school, homes, weather;
- drawing simple maps or making weather charts;
- examining various kinds of leaves or soil and noticing their differences;
- reporting back after a field-trip looking at local buildings or a nature site.

Juniors

Juniors are expected to explore more complex geographical concepts as they proceed through the school, such as:

- how to use a compass;
- being able to recognise map symbols on Ordnance Survey maps;
- understanding earthquakes and volcanoes;
- understanding erosion caused by rivers, waves and wind;
- knowing about different kinds of weather conditions, such as polar, temperate and tropical;
- understanding how land is used in different ways, e.g. farming, mining or building;
- understanding environmental issues such as pollution and over-mining.

In visiting the junior classroom you would expect to see children involved in activities such as:

- finding places on a globe or in an atlas;
- looking at large-scale Ordnance Survey maps;
- project work or topics such as the landscape in their local area or the study of a European country, the study of a location in a Third-World country, or a study of a local native site.

Home partnership

We can help the development of geographical skills by helping our children notice things in the local environment or look more closely at the places we visit on holiday, whether abroad or in Britain. We can encourage them to take a close look at the main features of a place, for example, trees, lakes, rivers, hills or the seaside. If we are on a beach, we can encourage them to look at the rock formation of the cliffs or the shape of the sand dunes and discuss how they came to be like that. If we are standing on a hill looking down into a valley, we can ask children how they think the land came to be like that, and why villages or towns are built in valleys.

Weather is a subject that comes up a lot in Britain. We can talk to our children about the impact weather has on the way people live and on the landscape around us.

We can encourage children to notice the direction in which they are travelling, whether this is on foot or by car or train, and see if they can tell us the way on simple routes, e.g. 'go past the garage', 'turn left by the church', etc.

We can buy a globe so they can understand the world is a sphere, the comparative sizes of different countries and continents, and how far away they are from the UK. There are puzzles made up of the different counties in the UK or games that involve travelling around the world, such as GO, which can teach children where different places are.

If you are going abroad on holiday, you can explore where your destination is on the map before you leave, and you can talk to your children about the different landscape, climate and customs of the place you are visiting.

The food we buy in our local supermarket has been imported from all around the world. When children come shopping, we can get them to look at the labels to see where in the world the food they are going to eat comes from and we can get them to look the places up on the map.

15

Development of design and technological skills

The modern world is a world of design. All around us the consumer society feeds on the design of clothes, home décor and lifestyle objects such as zany kitchen utensils, not to mention white goods and computer games. Many jobs are related to this world of competitive product design. Design and technology lessons give children the chance to explore and investigate how products and objects actually work and which tools are appropriate for which task. Children learn to build and put things together in a way in which problems are thought about and addressed, and different ways of solving them attempted. They explore a wide range of materials that can be used for different jobs, utilised and changed to suit the purpose in hand. They also look at how design and technology meet the need of a particular consumer or client group who will use the product. Children need encouragement to create their own ideas and test their creativity in reality.

School partnership

Design and technological skills will be interwoven in a cross-curricular way across most skill development areas, especially when children are concentrating on topic work such as historical or scientific exploration. The opportunities children have to explore their own design ideas will depend on the school's commitment to these kinds of kinaesthetic, practical activities. Cooking is now known as food technology and different dishes become 'products' and this is a part of technology that children particularly enjoy.

Schools will aim to develop some of the following:

- ideas for design and technology products and children being able to discuss their ideas, why they think they will work, and then make them, using a range of different materials such as paper, cardboard, wood and different textiles;
- a use of different tools and equipment such as glue, scissors, carpentry tools and kitchen cooking equipment;
- children being able to assemble materials and components in different ways;
- children being able to see the good design elements to their creation as well as being able to examine design flaws and discussing how they could make their product better.

Home partnership

We can help our children develop design and technological skills through encouraging their creativity and providing materials and activities that will promote these skills. Many children love either helping us to cook in the kitchen, chopping and preparing vegetables or whipping up cream. They can then progress to following a recipe and creating their own cooking ideas. They can decide what flavours or colours to use when making cakes and biscuits and then decorate them to make an appetising and inviting product (sometimes!).

Providing our children with building materials such as Lego, Knex and Meccano allows them to use different basic-building blocks to build different 'products' and to solve problems about how they will work best. There are many good creative children's packages on the market that involve putting pieces together to make a whole, e.g. model aeroplanes, and children can then design and paint the end product.

We can collect junk such as card, paper, balls of wool, old scraps of material, loo rolls and cereal boxes and allow children to get to work with scissors and glue to build things using their imagination. We can buy small-size carpentry tools and provide a workspace and some off-cuts of wood to allow children to saw and nail things together to make something of their own choosing.

We can also encourage our children to notice the materials being used in the world around them. Why are car tyres made from rubber? Why are houses made of brick? What is the difference between wood and metal, and why are some things made of wood and others from metal? By pointing out things to children, they begin to get an idea of the complexity and diversity of design around them.

16

Development of information and communication technology skills

We live in a world where every year brings huge movements forward in information and communication technology. It is essential that children, from a young age, get to grips with modern technology and how it is changing the way we live and work on an everyday basis. They need to be familiar with computers, keyboards, word processing, using the Internet and sending emails. They need to learn to use digital cameras, scanners and recording equipment, to programme videos, and to be able to access a range of computer software. Children need to know how to find information, store it for future use, share it with other people, and use it to match their particular need at the time. Luckily for the less technological among us parents, children take to modern technology like ducks to water!

School partnership

Schools are having to make more and more provision for the development of children's information and communication technology skills as these become the groundwork of much of their future learning and essential knowledge for the work placement. Many schools now have 'computer suites' where there are a roomful of computers that a whole class or group of children can come and work on at a given time. Most individual classrooms will have one or more computers at the side of the class for children to use.

The importance of learning keyboard skills cannot be over-emphasised. Increasingly in the workplace, everyone is expected to have some competency in word processing and in being able to manage basic computer skills.

Most children enjoy working on computers because they provide fast visual stimulus and children like the feeling of being in control. Schools develop children's skills on the back of this enjoyment.

Children will be learning skills such as:

- using ICT (information and communication technology) to handle information in different ways; gathering it, organising it, storing it and presenting it to others;
- using word-processing programmes to write and change class work;
- using graphics and sound to enhance their presentation;
- using programmable toys, putting together computerised instructions in the right order;
- doing mathematical games and problem-solving questions using software programmes;
- experimenting with design and presentation by using different styles and sizes of font or different colours;
- looking up information on the Internet;
- sending and receiving emails;
- using scanners to insert pictures and illustrations into text work;
- using videos and sound-recording equipment.

Home partnership

This is one area of the curriculum where children are often ahead of parents. Often children will be instructing us rather than the other way round! What we can do, is provide them with the equipment they need to develop their skills at home as well as at school. Although computer equipment is expensive, it is an investment well worth making as it is a skill area that will be so essential to your child's long-term future. A lot of computer skill comes from having the time to explore the machine's capabilities and experimenting with different techniques and ways of managing what can be done.

Computer time, while important, should be rationed – especially as some children have a tendency to become a bit obsessed with playing games and surfing the Net. There are many other pursuits more important to the health and welfare of children – for example, running around in the fresh air and making friends! It is best to have a computer in a general family area rather than in a child's bedroom. This is because children can become very isolated simply staring at the screen and also because of the dangers of unsuitable material on the Internet. It is best to have a computer where you can monitor what is going on.

Children can also have great fun with sound systems, tape recorders and cameras and other pieces of technological equipment. Increasingly, mobile phones are becoming an essential piece of hardware for every child to own (although these are not recommended for children, as it is not fully known what is the impact of long-term use on the developing brain). We can draw our children's attention to information and communication technology where we see it around us, as increasingly it becomes part of the modern world.

17

Development of musical awareness and musical composition

An appreciation and a love of music can provide a lifetime of enjoyment and pleasure, and so is a valuable resource in our children's lives. In order to appreciate music, recognise tunes and develop singing and instrumental talent, children need to be introduced to a wide range of musical skills and awareness. Making music together helps children to explore their thoughts and feelings and is both fun and enjoyable.

School partnership

Musical skills are an important part of what many schools have to offer. They provide a full range of opportunities for children to develop these skills, and will also give children an opportunity to develop and show off their musical talent through concerts or musical drama that are often highlights of the school year.

Infants

Young children have a natural affinity with music, rhythm and tune. They love listening to music, dancing to it, singing songs and playing a range of instruments. The infant classroom teaches the following skills:

- learning to listen attentively to music;
- recognising and being able to describe variations in sound, e.g. fast/slow, high/low or loud/quiet;
- singing, humming and clapping a song or tune;
- making simple percussion instruments and learning how to use them;
- making up a tune or rhythm with instruments;
- developing responses to music, identifying mood and feeling;
- developing preferences to music children like.

Examples of skills taught to older primary school children are:

Juniors

- an understanding of musical language, e.g. quavers and crotchets, and how they are represented in a musical score;
- an understanding of melody, accompaniment, chords, metre and rhythm;
- an understanding that there are a wide variety of styles and periods of music and how these can be identified through their 'sound';
- an understanding that there are different groups of instruments such as brass, wind and strings;
- an ability to listen to longer pieces of music and identify some instruments being used;
- the ability to compose a simple piece which has a beginning, a middle and an end;
- the ability to read and compose simple music scores;
- the learning of a musical instrument.

Home partnership

We develop our children's musical skills by exposing them to lots of different musical stimulus and experience. Simply listening to music develops musical awareness and skill. If we play different types of music at home then we can get children to notice these differences – how is classical music different from folk, jazz, pop or rock? This is how children can develop a taste for the music they like which is a personal preference. Let them develop this personal preference which may not be the same as yours!

Children find rhythm easier to follow when they connect it with some kind of physical movement. We can help our children feel rhythms through clapping along to the music, dancing to the music, or stamping feet in time to the music.

Children love singing along in accompaniment to musical songs. There are lots of excellent sing along tapes on the market for young children; older children may like the idea of karaoke tapes. Encourage your child to sing and find joy in singing.

In order to appreciate music, it is also necessary to appreciate the sound of silence. Silence is very important to music. You can help your children to become more aware of silence by encouraging them to listen to the kind of quiet background sounds that are heard when everything else is turned off – a bird singing in the garden, the sound of the wind in the trees, the sound of an aeroplane overhead, and so on.

Some children will want to learn a musical instrument. Many young children start off learning the recorder, piano or violin. Some schools will be able to offer individual or group tuition, or will know of someone in the local community who is prepared to offer this. Learning a musical instrument does require a commitment by parents to encourage practice and to boost confidence. It also means putting up with some inharmonious versions of scales and tunes! Learning a musical instrument requires a number of skills that improve children's concentration, listening, ordering and sequencing abilities. All skills that will be reflected in their general classroom ability.

Children need to experiment with making up compositions and 'playing' with music. Keyboards are a reasonable price and can also be picked up second-hand, and modern technology allows children to try out a range of harmony alternatives with different background rhythms.

Being able to read music is something children pick up very easily when young and it will give them lifelong pleasure in being able to sing or play an instrument. It also means that it is easier for them to begin learning another instrument when they go on to secondary education. If we read music ourselves, we can help our children build up skills in this area.

18

Development of creativity and artistic expression

Art and design is another way in which children can express themselves and communicate with others. Developing creative ways in which to express individuality, ideas and imaginative concepts is a vital part of all-round growth and learning potential. Through art and design children can show how they perceive the world by making a picture of what's around them and communicating how they feel through using different patterns, materials and textures.

Children today live in a rainbow-coloured, incredibly visual world with huge variations in artistic interpretation and design. One of the roles of skill development in this area is to enhance children's ability to notice what is in front of them.

School partnership

Good schools are careful to make a wide range of provision for artistic expression. There is a direct correlation between the standard of artwork around a school and its academic standards. Children who have opportunities to express themselves creatively and artistically are more likely to be happy and enthusiastic learners in other areas of the curriculum.

At primary school, children should have an opportunity to explore as many different mediums of expression as possible. This means having access to a comprehensive range of good-quality artistic materials. There should be a seamless join between more academic areas of skill development and artistic expression. Children can use art to express and reflect what they are learning in topics across the curriculum.

The kinds of skills which schools will be teaching will include the following:

Infants

- being able to use a range of different art materials for drawing, painting and making things;
- having an understanding of two-dimensional artwork (drawing and painting) and three-dimensional artwork (clay, junk-modelling);
- mixing colours to make other colours;
- using colour for effect;
- the ability to use broad and thin lines to define shape and form;
- learning to look at objects from different viewpoints;
- the ability to make comparisons between their own work and the work of well-known artists;
- being able to discuss the different designs of simple objects;
- being able to make their own designs for cards or three-dimensional objects, e.g. a rocket.

The kinds of activities you might observe in the infant classroom would include:

- children experimenting with paints using hands, feet, fingers and different sizes of brushes;
- children mixing paints;
- children drawing with crayons, pencils, felt pens and charcoal;

- children modelling things out of clay, plasticine or playdough;
- children making collages from pasta, shells, straw, feathers, wool, etc.;
- children making junk models out of old boxes and household-waste card and plastic.

Juniors

Juniors will be expected to move on from purely experiential expression to understanding some of the background skills required for artistic ability and appreciation. They will be developing some of the following concepts:

- an understanding of the roles of line, tone, colour and texture in artwork;
- an understanding of different kinds of design and visual forms in the media and environment, e.g. posters and advertisements;
- an appreciation of the design of costume, fashion and textiles;
- an increasing ability to look carefully at, and show some critical appreciation of, great artists' work;
- powers of observation and the ability to draw objects around them and in the wider environment;
- looking at things from a different perspective, e.g. a bird's-eye view, a view through a window or door, a view from a distance etc.;
- the ability to work in three-dimensions with clay to make simple objects.

These are the kinds of activities you might see in an art and design lesson in a junior classroom:

- children experimenting with printing;
- children sketching around the school from different vantage points;
- children drawing self-portraits or portraits of their classmates;
- children engaged in a design project to make something, working co-operatively with a group to solve problems.

Home partnership

As parents, we can complement our children's artistic development in a number of important ways.

We can provide them with opportunities to draw, paint and make things in the home environment. It is easy to find scrap paper, and pencils, felt pens and paints are not expensive. Keep a cardboard box with a variety of junk in it, such as loo rolls and cereal boxes so children can make 'junk' models with scissors and glue. Keep old magazines that children can cut up to make collages from different pictures. Little bits of textile materials left over from curtains, or cut up from old clothes, buttons and left-over lengths of wool, can all provide material from which children can create and re-make something from their own imagination. This can keep children busy, involved, but also learning.

If you have a garage or work space, then children also like building things out of scraps of wood and can be very proficient with tools from an early age if supervised and taught how to use them. Furniture designers have to start somewhere!

We can help children to observe things around them like colour, shape, form, space and symmetry and to appreciate how things look. We can help them to be more observant when looking at illustrations in story books, and ask them what they think is interesting or appealing about a particular illustration – why do we want to look at it?

How we receive our children's artwork will almost certainly have an effect on how they see themselves artistically. It is important to value their artistic offering in a positive and encouraging way. Many parents put their children's artwork up around the kitchen which signals that we gain pleasure and approve of their creative expression.

19

Development of physical competence and co-ordination

Education is about mind, *body* and spirit. It is only when all three are in place that we can operate at an optimum as human beings. Keeping fit, healthy and active is an essential for children's long-term well-being and development. Research studies have indicated that physical exercise can prove a key role in concentration and attention skills in the classroom. There is evidence to suggest that children who get into the habit of regular physical exercise, which they enjoy, will continue to see sport and fitness as important in later life with long-term implications for health and weight control. Today, many children are overweight or even obese. They spend many hours in front of a computer or television instead of running, playing and relating to other children outside.

For most children, exercise and sport are activities to be enjoyed – children are naturally keen to run around and use up their high levels of energy. Challenging and stretching their physical compe-tence and skill level is something that they have been doing ever since they first rolled over as babies. Unfortunately, in many schools, the sports curriculum has been seriously compromised over the last few years. School playing fields have been sold off for building development and after-school clubs and activities are more unusual due to teachers being less willing to give unscheduled time in running sporting events. Many children will not experience proper competitive team games until they attend secondary school. Therefore there is a greater onus on parents to 'fill the gap'.

School partnership

Primary schools concentrate on developing children's physical skills and competence in a number of different ways which will form the basis of most team and individual games, dance and gymnastics. Children will probably have around two hours of scheduled curriculum PE classes. Most schools will take children to the local swimming pool once a week to learn to swim and do basic strokes. Some schools will develop lunchtime or after-school clubs for football, dance or netball depending on how important the head teacher rates sporting activity and on the commitment of the staff. There is a major difference between the private and state sector in this area, with private schools putting a much greater emphasis on representing the school in sporting activities and competitive team games.

Children will be encouraged to develop the following skills during their primary school education:

- running over short and long distances;
- jumping high and long;
- throwing, catching, kicking and passing small and large balls with the aim of developing accuracy, speed and distance;
- hitting balls with a rounders bat, short tennis racket, etc.;
- gymnastic skills such as climbing, balancing, rolling and swinging;
- developing control, balance and poise through dance and dance sequences;

- becoming confident in water, being aware of water safety, and swimming on their fronts and backs with recognisable strokes.

Children are also developing the basis of team games such as:

- understanding and keeping to the rules of a team game;
- learning that the team must work together;
- developing 'fielding' skills.

On a visit to the primary school you might see:

- children doing athletic/PE activities inside or outside;
- big apparatus out in the hall with children learning different movements on each different piece;
- juniors playing team games such as football, netball and rounders;
- children developing dance sequences, capturing the mood of a piece of music;
- children on their way to the local swimming pool once a week.

Home partnership

There are many ways in which parents can encourage and play a part in the development of physical competence and sporting ability in children. We can start by simply kicking a ball around in the garden or by playing catch. We can take them to playgrounds with climbing equipment where they can test out their climbing abilities. Simple bat-and-ball games can improve children's hand–eye co-ordination which is the basis of so many games like tennis, squash, cricket and hockey.

There are now a wealth of sporting activities available in the local community. Local football, rugby, tennis and cricket clubs often have youth sections where adult club members give up time to train and encourage youngsters at weekends or in the evenings. There are dance, trampolining, martial arts, short tennis, swimming and badminton classes available in most leisure centres in the later afternoons and early evenings specifically for primary school children. These provide opportunities to learn new skills and make new friends outside the school environment.

Physical exercise and sport have a direct correlation with your child's ability to succeed at school simply because a healthy body balances a healthy, alert mind. Many activities such as dance or martial arts require a high level of sequencing and ordering that enable the brain to develop a way of processing information in a kinaesthetic way outside the classroom which will impact on skills such as mathematical ability.

If children see we have an interest in keeping fit, healthy and active ourselves, this will rub off on them in a positive way. Children enjoy doing things with their parents, so playing their favourite sport with them is a way to spend an enjoyable time as a family. The important thing is to find the activity your individual child enjoys participating in and has a flair for. Some children will prefer joining in with team sports such as football, others prefer the challenge of a more individual sport such as tennis or swimming. Some boys can become very fixated with a particular sport, and it is good to encourage them in other options so they develop skills apart from foot on the ball!

Many schools welcome parents prepared to run lunchtime or after-school clubs in a particular sport. So, if you have a talent in this area, how about putting something into the school community? If your child is selected to play in a match for their local team or school, then try to make the time to go and watch. Children really appreciate parents on the touch line cheering them on and it is another way of valuing their physical competence and skill.

20

Development of spiritual awareness and religious knowledge

Spiritual development is an important part of being a fully rounded human being. Spiritual awareness gives us a sense of being part of a bigger picture and a bigger world and universe which is full of mystery and things we don't fully understand. It gives us a sense of wonder at the beauty and diversity of the natural world as well as a sense of the supernatural beyond what we know scientifically or otherwise. It gives us the chance to explore what it means to be human and to develop beliefs and values that will be reflected in the way we relate both to and with others and the community in which we live.

In order to develop these beliefs and values, children need an opportunity to respond to the beliefs and values of others and to be encouraged to respect other people's choices while making choices for themselves.

School partnership

The development of spiritual awareness and religious knowledge will depend very much on the tradition, ethos and status of the individual school and the staff within it. If the school is a voluntary-aided Church of England or Catholic school, then there will be far greater emphasis on this part of the school curriculum. There may be an attachment to a local church where children regularly attend services. Some schools will hold services for parents and children at the beginning or end of every term. If this is important to you, then you need to investigate very carefully how children develop spiritually within the school and, in particular, the beliefs of the head teacher, as these are most likely to shape the worship and prayer of the compulsory assembly time.

In this country, religious education in school will reflect the fact that the religious traditions in Great Britain are mainly Christian, although they will also include teaching about other important religions that are becoming increasingly practised in a diverse, multi-cultural environment.

As a parent, you have a right to withdraw your child from assemblies and religious education lessons, although this might prevent them from developing discernment and understanding in making their own choices in later life.

These are the kinds of skills and learning that schools will be developing (at the child's level of understanding);

- an understanding of the Judeo–Christian concept of one God, and something of His nature;
- an understanding of the meaning of worship and prayer;
- the asking of spiritual questions – 'Who am I?', 'What is the meaning of life?' etc., and an understanding that this is a search humankind has always been on;
- a basic knowledge of the Christian faith and, in particular, the life, work, death and resurrection of Jesus Christ;
- a knowledge of some Bible stories;

- a knowledge of some Christian celebrations and what is the message behind them;
- a knowledge and understanding of Christian sacraments such as baptism and marriage;
- an understanding that different people have different ideas and beliefs about religion and spirituality;
- A knowledge of other world religions besides Christianity, such as Judaism, Islam, Hinduism and Buddhism, and how their traditions and customs differ.

Visiting the primary school you might observe some of the following:

- the school in an assembly, singing worship songs and saying simple prayers;
- simple Christian or humanistic messages being explained in an assembly through a teacher speaking, or children acting out stories and plays;
- Bible stories being read in assembly;
- children studying the stories, customs and traditions of other world religions through topic work, cooking and planned visits to different places of worship.

Home partnership

Your religious belief, faith or lack of it, will obviously greatly influence what you will teach and tell your children in reference to their spiritual development. An involvement in a faith community such as a church, synagogue or mosque will have an impact on how children acquire religious knowledge and spiritual awareness.

However, we can all encourage our children to have a sense of wonder at the natural world and to appreciate the diversity of life in all its beauty – a dazzling sunset, a ladybird sitting on their hand, or the multi-coloured fall of autumn leaves. We can also give them a moral humanistic framework to provide a reference point for right and wrong even if it does not come from a set of religious laws.

We can teach our children to respect a diversity of belief and encourage them to show tolerance and understanding of where other people place their faith, hope and beliefs.

Often, even if we are not regular churchgoers, in times of stress and grief or bewilderment, many of us will return to a belief in God, the after-life or at least a force for good against the evil of the world. What do we say to our children if there is a family death – do we encourage them to think of a loved one going to a better place or to heavenly realms? These are decisions we have to make as parents. Many of the important events in our lives such as births, weddings and deaths are intrinsically linked to visiting our local place of worship to mark these times 'standing in the presence of God'. Children also play a part in these events and need to have an understanding of age-old human traditions. They will also often ask awkward questions which challenge you and your beliefs, such as 'Who made the world?', 'Who is God?', 'Why do people die?', etc. Do you have your answers ready?

21

Development of personal, social and health education and citizenship

This is a big title for a complex range of skills, and basically means children learning to be independent and to develop a sense of self and self-worth that allows them to look after themselves and lead happy and healthy lives. These skills are hopefully being learned in an everyday way as part of your home and family life. Primary schools do not have to teach PSHE and citizenship, but the government is anxious that they encourage and underpin the curriculum with the beginning of these skills, so that they can be further explored during secondary education.

Children learn about their own rights, duties and responsibilities and the rights and responsibilities of others. They learn to show respect for other adults and children and to appreciate diversity and tolerance. They develop social skills, and they also learn about how to keep themselves healthy and safe through understanding hygiene, road safety, what and what not to eat, and knowing when to show caution and restraint. PSHE also teaches children about sex and relationships, and drugs and alcohol education.

School partnership

In the primary school, children will be exploring and developing personal skills such as:

- being more independent and confident with that independence;
- being able to identify and be proud of their strengths;
- having an awareness of areas they need to work on;
- being able to set goals and work towards them;
- having an idea of what is fair and unfair, or just or unjust;
- keeping themselves safe and healthy in a number of different ways.

They are also developing a social awareness of themselves as part of a peer group in relation to others. They will begin to:

- have an awareness of the kind of character and personality they have and how this impacts on others;
- know the kind of groups they want to belong to, and how they can contribute to them;
- have respect for, and be tolerant of, others.

Sex and relationship education

Every primary school has to provide a written statement about its sex and relationship education. This will tell you what is being taught, and at what age, and explain what the curriculum will cover. In the science National Curriculum, for example, children between the ages of five and seven will learn how all animals, including humans, reproduce.

Good schools will:

- consult parents on a regular basis when formulating their sex and relationships policy;
- complement what parents are doing at home;
- protect children from teaching or materials that are out of line

with their age, understanding or cultural background;
- teach that sex is best within a loving, long-term relationship.

The Education Act of 1996 gives you the right to withdraw your child from all or part of sex-education lessons. However, the law doesn't allow you to withdraw your child from the relevant aspects of science teaching.

Drugs education

In the early science curriculum, children will learn that some drugs can be good for the body and aid pain or fight disease (medicine) and that some drugs are dangerous to our bodies and against the law. As children get older, they will learn more about alcohol, smoking and drugs, the impact they have on the body, and the dangers of both prohibited and unprohibited substances.

Home partnership

PSHE skills are really about teaching our children skills that will enable them to manage their life both now, at home and at school, and in the future, when they become independent adults. Children learn to feel good about themselves and ambitious about who they are and what they can do through the positive feedback we give them. Children learn rights and responsibilities through the way we manage our families, and that although they have a right to be treated kindly, loved, looked after and cared for with a roof over their head and food on the table, they also have responsibilities towards others in the family. Children learn how to be healthy and safe but the signals we give them throughout the day, from washing their hands after going to the toilet to eating a variety of different foods like fruit and vegetables, are important.

We build children's self-esteem and self-worth by giving them plenty of praise and encouragement. We need to notice the little achievements and steps forward as well as the larger ones. We need to value trying as well as succeeding. Children need praise like flowers need water. Confidence will have a direct impact on your child's success at school because if children are confident they will be able to face the challenge and the risk which all kinds of learning involves.

Being good at something is a great motivator, not only in the particular area of gifting or talent but also in the way this core belief, 'I'm good at something', can spill over into other areas of learning. As a parent, it is very important to seek out things your child can excel in and enjoy, whether this is something in or outside school, and allow them to focus on it and have as much opportunity as possible to shine at it. This might not necessarily be a 'school subject'; it might be being good at singing, dancing, a particular sport, telling or writing stories, drawing or building things out of Lego. We need to follow our child's own interests and capabilities rather than trying to put a round peg into a square hole with interests of our own. Always remember developing skills is a process and the process may not proceed in a regimented, evenly spread time-span.

We can teach our children that everyone makes mistakes and gets things wrong and that this is part of the process of learning new things. We can explain that no one is good or competent at everything. We can help this process by admitting when we don't know, have got it wrong, or have failed ourselves. This helps children not to be frightened of failure, but to accept it as part of being on the road to where we want to go. It allows them to take risks without fearing the consequences of failing. It makes them believe that you can pick yourself up after a mistake and start again. It creates a robust sense of self-esteem.

We can lead by example, by showing our children that working hard and applying oneself can make a difference. Not everything in life is interesting and stimulating, and sometimes we just have to buckle down and get on with things, even if they are boring, in order to reach an end product. Give children positive feedback when they stick at things without giving up.

Even though they are small, children can gradually learn to support us with the practical everyday things that families need to do to live. This might involve doing household chores, learning to save their pocket money to buy birthday or Christmas presents for family members, or keeping their bedroom tidy. Chores that children can do will change as they get older and more capable, but will always give them a sense of responsibility and ownership and a feeling that they are a member of a group working together. They also encourage them to be willing to help and show consideration towards others. This must be balanced by allowing them to have a childhood too, so the chores should be age-appropriate and leave room for play and other activities!

Children enjoy helping prepare and make meals, chopping vegetables and stirring things in saucepans. They are often not so keen on clearing up! Through getting them to wash, dry up and put things away, or help to fill and empty the dishwasher they are learning that activities have downsides as well as upsides!

Teaching children to be healthy and safe comes about primarily by the example we give to our children. How we eat, keep clean, are careful with electrics, fire and dangerous substances will show them how to behave. We also have to be aware of their inexperience and give them clear instructions and warnings on what is and isn't a threat to their safety. Teaching road safety, for example, is a life-and-death business.

We can also give children examples of community-wide responsibility by becoming involved in community or environmental projects that allow them to see they do have a voice and a chance to change things even on a small local scale.

We need to teach children to have respect for their own bodies and be able to look after themselves as independently as possible. Children need to understand how their bodies work and how they are kept healthy and clean. They need to learn about personal space and touch and what is and isn't appropriate with different people.

Sex and relationships education

Talking to your children about sex and relationships is a personal and private business, but it is worth knowing when and what the school will be teaching your child so that you are aware when questions might come up and be ready to answer them. There are really two sides to talking to children about sex and relationships – the biological reality and outcomes of sexual intercourse and the relationship side of love, care and physical closeness – and, as parents, we must try to interweave both into our conversation with children.

There are some very good books on the market which can help you to explore the subject of 'where babies come from' with excellent illustrations and using language that children can understand. As a basic rule of thumb it is best to wait until your child asks you a question about sex before launching into a biology lesson. Try to answer truthfully but within the range of the child's capability to understand. Many children, particularly girls, may approach or begin puberty before they leave primary school, so it is important to have thought through our approach to the subject and prepare them for what will be happening to their bodies.

Pre-adolescent children are in many ways easier to talk to about sex and relationships because they can look at the subject in a more distant objective way rather than teenagers who have entered the world of wild hormones and embarrassment about relating to the other sex.

Drugs education

If we want our children to make good choices in later life, then we have to start educating them from an early age on the impact of different substances on the body and on the lives of people around them. If we, as parents, misuse tobacco, alcohol or take prohibited drugs, we are normalising behaviour that is dangerous and abusive to the health of our children and increasing the likelihood that they will do the same things in their teens and adult life. This misuse will also have a profound impact on our parenting.

We can complement the work that schools do in this area by being informed ourselves about different substances – legal and illegal – their street names, and how young people perceive and use them. Some schools will get someone to talk to the parents about the drugs education they are offering and give them some complementary training. This will give us a head start in credibility with our children. They will be able to tell that we are clear-headed and logical rather than acting with a blanket huge anxiety and worry that does not allow for discussion. Many children are involved in underage drinking with their peer group, even from the age of ten, so alcohol is something that needs to be talked about within the home. Children need to understand the virtue of moderation and things can be enjoyed but also controlled and managed in such a way as not to cause harm to themselves and other people.

22

Problems and solutions – home and school working together

Work worries

We know, as parents, that our children are in school to do school work. This in itself can produce worries and raise parental anxiety levels. Can they do the work that is being given them? Do they understand it and what can they do if they don't understand it? What happens if they fall behind?

One of the most important things we can explain to our children is that the best thing to do when you are struggling or don't understand something, is to ask for help. The ability to ask for help when necessary will help our children progress, whatever their underlying competence. Some children have no difficulty in asking for help and will stay with that help until they fully understand what it is they have to do. Other children will assume that they understand and then find out they don't, but plough on, making a hash of what they have to do. Some children know they don't understand, but feel it is a personal climb-down to ask for help.

They then miss out on the basic building blocks of learning a particular topic and as time goes on, they may get left further and further behind.

Children need to know that not everyone knows everything. We are all in the process of trying to learn and understand new things throughout our lives. There is no shame in taking risks and making mistakes. That is often how we learn more.

Special learning needs

Many children will have a special learning need at some time during their school career and will need to have some extra support and help to access and keep up with the curriculum. Primary schools are set up to cope with children within a wide band of ability and have a responsibility to integrate all children within their local community. The only children who may have to go to a special school are children with serious mental and physical delay or profound physical difficulties.

All schools are required to have a teacher who acts as a Special Needs Co-ordinator. This teacher is in charge of monitoring all youngsters who have any kind of special need that may affect their ability to access the National Curriculum. This could be a learning difficulty in the area of literacy (dyslexia) or numerary (dyscalculia), hearing or visual impairment, emotional and behavioural difficulties, physical disability, or a wide range of medical or neurological conditions. The government has given schools a 'Code of Practice for Special Educational Needs' which gives detailed advice as to how pupils should be monitored and supported in every school environment depending on the extent of their need. Extra money is given to schools to enable them to support pupils and different schools will choose to spend this money in different ways.

Sometimes, a child will need one-to-one help or to be part of a small group instead of a whole class for some of the time. It can also be important that work is what is called differentiated (same subject, or learning topic, but adjusted to a level the child can cope with). This means children can still participate in what is going on and retain their self-esteem moving at their own pace.

Some children, whose special educational needs are of particular concern, will need to be seen by an educational psychologist who will assess the ways an individual child thinks and learns in great detail. Children can be referred directly to an educational psychologist by parents, or in partnership with the school. The educational psychologist will spend some time getting a full learning background and pinpointing the precise difficulties the child is experiencing. Part of this process will involve talking to parents about their worries and concerns and taking an early history of the child's development that might prove helpful. Usually, educational psychologists will keep in touch with schools and monitor a child's progress. They will give specific advice on how a child might be helped to overcome their difficulties.

Some youngsters will have difficulties that require support beyond the normal financial resources of the school. If, after initial advice has been taken and support given, a child fails to progress in the way the school and parents have hoped then a 'Statement of Special Educational Needs' might be necessary. This is a legal document that gives the child a statutory (legal) right to a range of provision extra to normal school resources. In this case, the educational psychologist, or other agencies outside the school, will recommend a 'multi-disciplinary' assessment of the child's physical, social and mental abilities. The outcome of this assessment will be clear recommendations of the type of support the child needs and should have access to.

Parental views are sought and respected throughout the process of 'statementing'. Parents have a right to ask for certain resources to be made available to their child, and are able to challenge the view of the LEA if they disagree with the outcome of the statement. For example, if the LEA suggests that a child with a statement should attend their local comprehensive, but the parents feel that this school would not meet their child's needs, then, as set out in the terms of the statement, they have a right of appeal to a Special Needs tribunal. Some parents have successfully challenged

LEAs and have exercised their right to choose an Independent Special School that, in their opinion, better meets their child's need.

If you suspect your child has some kind of special need or learning difficulty, it is good to check this out with your child's class teacher. The sooner any difficulties are picked up, the sooner something can be done about them and the right help given.

Gifted or very intelligent children

Some children are exceptionally bright and intelligent and easily outstrip their peer group in being able to do their school work. This can be particularly true with mathematics. These children have a special need as well, and need to be challenged and given work that will promote their full development potential. Sometimes, children who are under-stimulated become bored and consequently disruptive in the classroom. If you think your child may be exceptionally bright (please try to be realistic!), then you need to discuss with the school how they are going to meet his or her needs.

Competition

The world is a competitive place and schools have their competitive side as well. Due to the demands of SATs and league tables, primary schools have become increasingly focused on academic attainment and achievement for their pupils. This focus has made children increasingly aware of the world of competition. As they proceed up primary school they become alert to 'marks' and are able to make comparisons as to success and failure in pieces of work. They will know how they have done in tests and SATs and either be proud of their achievement and have a healthy self-confidence, or feel that they have not made the grade and are 'failing'. How can we help them deal with the competitive side of schooling?

First, we must be aware of our own competitiveness for our children and beware of living vicariously through their achievements! Sometimes, parents are more competitive about their children than children are for themselves! This may be to do with your own achievement or lack of achievement at school and getting another 'chance' through your children – watch out for this. Remember, your child is an individual with his or her own talents and gifts, as well as things to struggle with. You may be encouraging a competitive edge to your child, but also promoting anxiety and worry that they may not be able to meet your high expectations.

Your focus on your child's reports should be on what they have done well and the achievements they have attained, rather than on what could be done better or your disappointments about their competence in a certain area. Let them know that you are proud of what they have actually achieved rather than laying emphasis on what they might achieve.

As parents, we cannot protect our children from comparisons or the reality that they are not the 'best' at everything. However, if we value all their strengths, not just the academic, we allow them to see that everyone has their own area of gifting and potential whatever that maybe. None of us are good at everything.

School refusal

Many children find it hard to cope with the school routine when they first start school and may show a reluctance to go to school some mornings. There are many bewildering adjustments to make and it will take time for them to settle in. However, some children may continue to be reluctant to go to school after quite a few terms or suddenly become reluctant to go to school pleading illness like stomach aches, nausea or headaches. This could indicate a problem that needs sorting out. This could involve one of the following:

Physical illness

If you feel it necessary, take your child to the doctor and have them checked out physically – sometimes there really are physical reasons behind some of these symptoms which seem psychosomatic in nature. Children can get low-level viral infections, M.E. and glandular fever, that can cause them to be run down for months.

Bullying

A frequent reason for school refusal is a simmering or more virulent bullying problem within the classroom or in the playground. The next section deals with bullying in greater depth.

Difficulties with friendships

Sometimes, children will be reluctant to go to school because they are finding it difficult to make friends or join in with groups in the playground. They may just have had some kind of argument with a friend or friends the day before and are worried as to whether they will be able to sort it out. If you think your child is having problems socially, then it is worth talking to the class teacher for his or her observations as to how they are getting along. See chapter 5 for further insight.

Personality clash with the teacher

Sometimes, a child will suffer from having a personality clash with a particular teacher. Teachers are flawed human beings, the same as anyone else, and will sometimes, in what is a totally unprofessional manner, take against a particular child. Your child might complain at getting picked on or punished unnecessarily, or being shouted at by the teacher. You need to try to sort this out by not becoming aggressive or defensive yourself but by quietly trying to address the teacher with the problem. You could say that your child feels that they are not able to do anything right within the classroom and it is making them unhappy. How can you help the teacher to turn things around? If you do not feel that you are making any headway, then remain calm but refer to the head teacher, putting your case with some clear examples of what you feel are unprofessional comments towards your child.

Sometimes, a teacher's personality will not suit your child very well – maybe the teacher is loud and brash and your child is sensitive and quiet. However tough this is, children have to adapt to the difficult personalities of the world and will sometimes have to 'bite the bullet' and keep their heads down, hoping they will get a nicer teacher next time round.

Concentration difficulties

Some children do find it very difficult to concentrate, preferring activity to concentration. They are often easily distracted, and tend to think before they act. If your child is like this, then he or she may find it extremely hard to settle at school and find themselves in constant trouble for their behaviour. This might be because they are wandering around the classroom rather than sitting still, chatting rather than working, or fiddling with things rather than listening. They then become reluctant to go to school because the demands for concentration and listening are perceived by the child as being too great for them to manage. (See chapters 6 and 8.)

Learning difficulties

If children are struggling with the complexity of the work being given them, and feel they cannot achieve what is being expected of them, they can lose confidence and not want to go to school. It is important to work with the school in making sure that the work is adjusted (differentiated) so that your child can manage it, and to work in partnership with the Special Needs Co-ordinator to ensure they get sufficient support.

Jealousy of younger sibling

When there is a new baby in the house, or younger children at home, some older siblings may not want to come to school because they think they are missing out on all the attention and fun. They need to be persuaded that they are not forgotten when they are at school and perhaps they will be doing special and fun things at school that their young sibling cannot join in with!

Anxiety about what will happen at home

If you are struggling with major issues at home such as bereavement, separation or divorce, domestic violence, money worries, substance misuse or mental or physical illness, then your child may become reluctant to go to school as they do not want to leave you because they are worried what might happen to you while they are at school.

Seek help for yourself when possible and always try to communicate the truth to your child in as much as they can understand things according to the age and level of maturity they are at. Reassure them that Mum or Dad will cope and the best thing they can do is go to school and be with their friends where they will be busy and learning things.

School phobia

Very rarely, a child may become phobic about going to school. It may begin with one of the above difficulties, but then become so all-encompassing that the child will become extremely distressed at even the thought of going to school. You must then seek help from a child psychologist who can help you rebuild your child's confidence and work with the school to help get them back to school, even if only on a staggered basis.

Bullying problems

Most of us can remember incidents at school when we witnessed bullying, were bullied, or bullied someone at school. Being bullied can be an extremely painful experience and its effects can last a lifetime. Despite school initiatives to combat bullying, there still remains a high incidence of bullying behaviour, both in primary and secondary schools. Bullying can lead to poor school performance across the curriculum, stress, anxiety, depression, poor self-esteem and confidence. In order to help our children be successful at school, we need to protect them as far as we can from being bullied, feeling the need to bully or being part of a bullying environment. We need to work in partnership with schools to 'bully-proof' both the environment and our child.

What is bullying?

Bullying includes some kind of deliberate hostility and aggression towards another person. The victim of the bullying usually appears weaker and less powerful than the bully or bullies for one reason or another. The outcome is always painful and distressing for the child being bullied.

Bullying can take many different forms. Bullying can be physical – for example, pushing, kicking, hitting, pinching and any other forms of violence or physical threat; boys tend to be more involved in physical types of bullying. Bullying can be verbal – for example, name-calling, sarcasm, spreading rumours or persistent teasing, even after being asked to stop; girls tend to be more involved in verbal types of bullying. Bullying can also be emotional – for example, exclusion, isolation or 'sending to Coventry'. It also can include tormenting others by hiding property, taunting, ridicule or humiliation.

Who are the victims of bullying?

Children who bully will find something about the victim child to focus on. Whatever it is, the so-called difference is just an excuse that the bully needs or creates to 'justify' his or her behaviour. As Adrian Mitchell's poem 'Back in the Playground Blues' goes:

> Well you get it for being Jewish,
> And you get it for being black,
> Get it for being chicken,
> And you get it for fighting back,
> You get it for being big and fat,
> Get it for being small,
> Oh those who get it get it and get it
> For any damn thing at all.

This means that any child can become vulnerable and a focus of bullying. The 'difference' is not the victim's fault. Bullying never is, and should never be assumed to be, the fault of the victim. In a perfect world, school environments should be created where differences are always appreciated and all children feel valued. Many schools try to work towards these worthy principles.

However, in an imperfect world, we would be foolish not to recognise that some children may be vulnerable to bullying because they have long-term or short-term specific problems. This might include children with special educational or physical needs; children under stress due to family difficulties such as divorce, separation, unemployment or financial problems; children with low self-esteem, or youngsters who are being bullied in the home by siblings or other family members. These children need extra protection and support to ensure their right to emotional and physical safety.

How can we spot possible signs of bullying?

If our child is being bullied they will begin to show certain symptoms of stress and/or emotional distress that we should pay attention to, and investigate the reasons behind, as soon as possible.

- A bullied child might become increasingly reluctant to go to school. This might manifest itself in feeling ill in the morning with headaches or stomach aches. Difficulties in getting up, trouble getting ready for school in the morning, or refusing to eat breakfast, might also be symptomatic of an underlying problem. This might particularly be the case if these things never happen at weekends or during the holidays.
- A bullied child may seem frightened to go to school and become either withdrawn or tearful prior to going.
- A bullied child may start having difficulty in getting to sleep, be tearful and weepy before bedtime, or have nightmares or night-waking. Some children will start to wet the bed again, having been dry for a number of years.
- A bullied child may begin to under-perform in their school work and their literacy and numeracy skills drop away.
- A bullied child may become withdrawn, start stammering, lack confidence or seem to be undergoing a personality change.
- A bullied child may become increasingly distressed, anxious or jumpy.
- Children who are being bullied at lunchtime often find it difficult to eat, and their lunch box will come home untouched.
- Sometimes, bullied children will ask for extra money or money will disappear from your purse. Possessions may continually go missing. Children may give improbable excuses to explain missing items.
- Be alert to unexplained bruises, scratches and cuts, particularly when children will not tell you how they happened.

What not to do if you think your child is being bullied

- Don't become aggressive towards the child or children who are bullying your child, or towards their parents.
- Don't act in an aggressive way towards the school, even if you feel they are not doing enough to sort out the problem.
- Don't tell your child to hit or hurt the bully – this rarely sorts the problem out.

- Don't tell your child that bullying is a normal part of growing up and it will toughen them up.
- Don't tell your child to sort themselves out or that a 'bit of teasing' will be the making of them – it won't.

What to do if you think your child is being bullied

- Keep calm and try to find out as much information as you can.
- Ask your child directly if they are being bullied. Be prepared for your child to deny what is happening at first, as he or she may be anxious or frightened of telling you. This might be because they are worried about your potential reaction of anger and be upset, or worry, about what you might do. Some children will feel a sense of shame that they can't sort out the problem themselves. Some children will feel that to admit to the problem is to enlarge it and make it even bigger in their mind. Some children think that they won't be believed. Some children have been threatened with dire consequences if they tell. Encourage your child by saying that you are concerned and want to help.
- Always take what your child says seriously and try to find out exactly what is going on. Believe your child's story, while keeping in mind there may be another one. Do not promise to keep the bullying secret, but reassure your child that you will help them sort out the problem.
- Go into the school and make an appointment with the class teacher and seek their support in addressing the bullying. If you have tried this and nothing has happened, then make an appointment with the head teacher. Get a copy of the school's anti-bullying policy and check if they are following their laid-down procedures in your child's case. If they are not, get in touch with a parent governor.
- If you discover your child is being bullied because they have an obnoxious habit such as picking their nose, then help them to change this habit. If they are being bullied because they have a 'sad' haircut this is something you can help with almost instantly. If you are the parent of a fat child, then start to change their

diet. Totally unfair as it is, the reality is that fat children are notoriously bullied for most of their school lives.

- Reassure your child that it is not their fault they are being bullied. Assure them that this is not right, fair or just that bullying is allowed to go on, nor is it right that bullies get away with such appalling behaviour.

- Encourage them that, with your support and help, they can take steps to make it stop. They are not helpless and powerless and things can be done to address the bullying. Urge them not to give up.

- It is essential to try to explain to your child that bullies want a payback for their cruel behaviour. The payback is a scared, cowered, frightened or angry reaction from their victim. Train your child not to react to the bullies' taunts. If bullies cannot see a reaction in their chosen victims, bullying becomes boring and they usually give up. Encourage your child to laugh at or ignore comments or teasing. Bullies want a scared reaction, and silence or humour makes you not worth bullying.

- Practise strategies with your child so that they can confidently use them if bullying occurs. If the strategy is to walk away, then discuss where to. If the strategy is to tell someone, then whom should they tell, etc. Help your child to become proficient at 'fogging'. This is when someone says, 'You're a pig', and you say, 'So you think I'm a pig?' or 'so that's your opinion, is it?' or something similar. This gets boring for the bully because there is no pay off.

- Children can gain in confidence through attending martial arts or self-defence courses. This does not mean necessarily fighting back but feeling that you could fight back if you wanted to.

- Children need to know to stay in a crowd; bullies are more likely to pick on loners.

- Help your child to be assertive and articulate their needs in front of witnesses. Get them to practise at home or in front of the mirror, telling the bullies to buzz off or shouting 'No' or 'Go Away'. Say it angrily and walk away immediately. Making eye contact with the weakest member of a bullying gang and saying,

'I don't like this' or 'This is wrong' can undermine the cohesion of the bullying gang.

- Keep a dated diary of events and incidents as your child reports them. Include any symptoms of stress, anxiety or depression that you have noticed. This can help to identify when and where your child is at most risk of bullying and provide firm evidence for schools.

- Use plenty of praise and affection to build up your child's self-confidence as this may have been considerably damaged if the bullying has been going on for some time. If your child seems to be bullied wherever they go, study how your child reacts to people. They may lack self-confidence, assertive skills or social skills. They may have difficulty getting into games or being part of their peer group activities. These difficulties may have been engendered by the initial bullying, but then perpetuate a cycle that is repeated again and again.

- Reassure your child that you love them and will always support them one hundred per cent. Encourage them to always tell you or an adult they can trust if they are being hurt or upset. You are on their side and can help.

What to do if your child is being a bully

Children who are bullies will ultimately be unpopular with their peer group and their desire for manipulative power and control over others can undermine their success at school both in performance and social terms. The behaviour can often be seen as symptomatic of a child's own insecurity and lack of self-confidence, leading them to feel the need to be superior to others by undermining them. They may feel insecure, inadequate or humiliated in some way. They may be under pressure to succeed at all costs. Some, however, are used to getting their own way all the time and like the feeling of power that engendering misery in others brings.

Most children can be capable of bullying behaviour at some time in their life. Some children become temporary bullies after traumatic events, such as a divorce, the birth of a new baby, a bereavement, a house or school move, or because they are struggling with school work. However, bullying behaviour can become habitual if it is not addressed very quickly, and children can develop into long-term chronic bullies who grow up to bully and harass people in adult life.

- If another parent or the school informs you that your child has been bullying another child, then try to remain calm and not become too defensive. If there is some truth in it, then you need to address it as soon as possible. Talk to teachers, dinner staff and friends who can give you more information. Reassure your child that you love them and will help them even if they have been badly behaved. However, they do need to tell you the complete truth so it can be sorted out.
- It is only right that a child should feel ashamed if they have been involved in shameful behaviour. This is part of the development of a conscience and a sense of morality. As a parent, you should communicate your sadness and disappointment at their bullying behaviour and make clear that bullying is a totally inappropriate way to behave. Set realistic, firm guidelines and rules to help your child control their behaviour. Ensure that your child apologises, either in person or in writing, to the child they bullied.
- Remember that children should have a clean slate as soon as possible after behaviour has been dealt with and punished. Children need to achieve some success to make them feel good about themselves. Help your child to find something they can do well, and often the behaviour will change.
- If you suspect your child is turning into a chronic bully, seek help. Speak to an educational psychologist or get a referral through your GP to see a child psychologist.

Emotional and behavioural difficulties

Sometimes, parents are called into schools to be told that their child is behaving inappropriately on a regular basis. This may involve disrupting the class process through talking or disturbing other children working. It might involve not getting on with their work, failing to listen or concentrate. There may be more serious concerns about a child being extremely attention-seeking, aggressive to others, bullying, swearing, being rude to teachers or damaging school property.

This is always distressing and upsetting for parents, and some see it as a direct judgement on their ability to parent or discipline their child by the school. Try to keep calm and remember that the school also want to help and support your child to behave appropriately, and, if you work in partnership with them, this is much more likely to happen. Most behavioural problems can be overcome through understanding why the behaviour might be happening and by putting together a plan to help the child change their behaviour in a systematic and consistent way.

Schools

Behaviour does not happen in a vacuum. Children will respond to the environment in which they find themselves. If the school does not have a clear, positive behaviour-management policy with clear expectations, incentives and boundaries, some children may find it difficult to behave appropriately. Some teachers have less control over their classroom than others, because of their underlying skills in being able to manage children. This may have an effect on the overall behaviour within the classroom.

Schools do have a duty to set up systems in which positive behaviours are encouraged and also to show understanding and commitment to children who are finding it hard to behave appropriately. One of the ways they do this is by letting you as a parent know what is going on and offering you the opportunity to work with them in changing things for the better. They will not want your child to fail to learn or under-achieve at school because of their behaviour. They also clearly have a duty to protect other children from behaviour that might interrupt their learning or affect their emotional or physical well-being.

Home

Behaviour does not happen in a vacuum. Children will respond to the environment in which they find themselves. If home does not have a clear positive behaviour-management policy with clear expectations, incentives and boundaries, some children may find it difficult to behave appropriately. Some parents have less control over their children than others, because of their underlying skills in being able to manage them. This may have an effect on their overall behaviour both at home and in school.

Parents do have a duty and a responsibility to encourage positive behaviour both at home and at school, and to work with other adults dealing with a child to ensure a consistent approach.

You will not want your child to fail to learn, or to under-achieve at school because of their behaviour. As a parent, you also clearly have a duty to protect other children from behaviour that might interrupt their learning or affect their emotional or physical well-being.

I hope the above has convinced you that parents and schools share the same goals when it comes to behaviour!

When we are trying to deal with behaviour, it is important to try to understand your child's feelings and 'where they are coming from'. Children who are always getting into trouble for their behaviour do not feel good about themselves. They may be trying to change their behaviour but somehow it doesn't seem to work. Adult intervention is necessary to help children to change and move on.

The first thing we have to do is to investigate why the behaviour might be happening. This could be for a number of reasons.

Personality/temperament

Some children just are more difficult to raise than others. They tend to be more self-willed and defiant than their brothers and sisters and demand more attention and parenting to keep them on an even keel. They just seem to be born that way. They may have a sibling who is never any problem, does as they are told, and is passive and complaint. We are all unique, individual human beings with our own personality and temperament and parents and teachers have to adapt to this just as children have to adapt to us and our ways.

Physical need

Sometimes children will behave badly because of a basic physical need: they are very tired, having stayed up too late, or having not slept well; they have low blood sugar and are hungry or dehydrated and thirsty; they could be feeling too hot and bothered, or too cold; they could be off-colour and feeling run-down, or coming down with some kind of infection. All these basic needs can affect the way we behave.

Feelings of self-esteem

Most children who are behaving badly will have a lack of self-confidence and self-esteem. The negative experience of adults nagging and telling them off constantly for the way they behave creates a downward spiral in which the child begins to believe the labels attributed to them, and the poor behaviour thus becomes a self-fulfilling prophecy. Adults need to help children break this pattern and turn things around so children can be 'caught being good', even if this is for small things such as putting clothes on when asked.

Physical or learning difficulty

Sometimes behavioural difficulties can be rooted in physical or learning difficulties. The child may have a hearing or language difficulty that is causing frustration or a lack of understanding of expectations or instructions. For example, if the child has a hearing difficulty, they may not be hearing most of what the teacher is saying. These problems can be checked out medically or, in the case of language disorders, with the help of a speech therapist.

Some children may be immature in their general development and therefore find it hard to meet the behavioural expectations of their peer group.

Some children who have literacy difficulties become more and more aware of the discrepancies between themselves and other members of the class in being able to read and write. If they are also bright and articulate, this can be extremely frustrating because it can be assumed you don't know the answers because you have difficulty writing them down. Some dyslexic children will start to be attention-seeking and behave badly to compensate for their difficulty.

Neurological conditions

Sometimes children may have an undiagnosed neurological condition. Children who have extremely poor attention skills and are 'all over the place' could be suffering from Attention Deficit Hyperactivity Disorder (ADHD). These are likely to be colic-troubled babies who don't sleep, and who grow into hyperactive, restless toddlers who subsequently become primary school children who have huge difficulties in meeting the concentration and attention demands of the classroom.

Some children who have severe problems with social skills and struggle with understanding others' personal space and body language may be on the 'autistic' continuum and need professional expert help and diagnosis.

There are other syndromes that medical professionals are becoming far more adept at diagnosing and can cause children to have considerable difficulties in behaving in the school arena.

It is also worth remembering that these conditions remain very rare and it is far more likely that you child's behaviour is part of their general growth and development.

Family issues

What happens within the family will affect family members and their behaviour. Children can be barometers of their parents' emotional life – they react and respond to our distress, sadness, depression or anger and can play it out in their own lives, sometimes at school. Separation and divorce, the birth of a new baby, a death in the family, domestic violence within the home, parents drinking too much or taking drugs, or abusive behaviour towards children will all have a profound affect. When a child is worried, anxious, angry or depressed, they can lash out to deflect their own pain on other people by becoming rude, aggressive or a bully.

Lack of skills

Sometimes it is children's lack of social skills or concentration and attention skills that get in the way of them being able to behave appropriately and then we have to think about giving them a boost in these areas.

What to do

Why is the behaviour happening?
First of all, you need to ask some questions about the behaviour that your child is showing. These might include:

- What exactly is the behaviour you are concerned about? What is it that you would like the child to do differently?

- Are there triggers to the behaviour that you can recognise? When, where and for how often do they happen? Sometimes keeping a diary for a few days both at home and at school can highlight a pattern of danger periods for your child.
- When did the behaviour start? Is there anything significant about the start date in terms of other events happening in the family or at school?
- Has you child always been a bit of a trouble-bubble or is this new?
- Have you been worried, distracted or depressed yourself by problems at any time during their childhood, or are you at this present time? Could your difficulties be having an impact on your child?
- Does your child behave differently at home and at school or are they much the same in terms of behaviour wherever they are?
- Are you worried that you don't have much control over your child's behaviour and that you need some help and support to gain your parental authority?

Ask for help

The next thing to do is to ask for help from other people to make a plan for change:

- If there are family issues, can you ask for some help from your GP or other agencies to gain support? We all need help sometimes and there is no shame, only sense, in seeking help where it is available. People outside the direct situation can see things more clearly than families caught up in the middle of the difficulty.
- With behavioural problems in school, parents and teachers working as a team can make a supportive combination when it comes to making positive changes. They can combine together to develop strategies to modify behaviour and rebuild a child's picture of himself or herself.
- Grandparents, family and close friends can also give you insight and support. The vast majority of parents have struggled with

some kind of behavioural problem with one of their children and they may have used effective strategies that could also work with your child.

- If you suspect there may be an underlying physical, learning or neurological difficulty that needs addressing, then ask for a referral to an educational psychologist or a medical consultant.

- The best way to change a child's behaviour is through the old-fashioned 'carrot and stick' method. This means choosing one to three target-behaviours that you want the child to change and, after making clear your specific expectations, giving them the opportunity to make good or bad choices with clear consequences for both. For example:

Teacher and parent working together

Behaviour
Child constantly out of seat disturbing others in classroom.

What we want to happen
Child being able to stay in seat when asked to, and to get on with their work.

Teacher and parent expectation
'We want you to stay in your seat in the classroom when you have been told to.'

Good consequence
'You will get a smiley sticker on your chart each school session when you stay in your seat. Then when you have ten smiley stickers in school, Mum will take you on a trip to the cinema.'

Bad consequence
'If you disturb the class by getting up out of your seat, then you will miss five minutes playtime.

The good and bad consequences need to be planned with the particular child in mind – what is it that will motivate your child, and what is a consequence that they will care about?

Children respond to positive attention – they want and need our approval. When they know they are going to get it, they can modify their behaviour.

By giving them choices, we are training them to understand that there are good and bad choices to be made with different outcomes and consequences.

Behavioural difficulties do not change overnight. They require persistence and consistency from the adults working with the child. A 'star chart' technique may be useful in breaking the pattern of habitual behaviour, but the child will still need long-term support and positive feedback to keep to the new habit of behaviour. Look back at chapter 6, which relates to the development of behavioural skills, for further ideas and guidance.